TWELVE AMERICAN POETS

# Twelve American Poets

EDITED BY

Stephen Whicher and Lars Åhnebrink

New York   OXFORD UNIVERSITY PRESS

*Twelve American Poets* was published in Sweden in 1959 in a slightly different form.

Selections from works by the following poets were made possible by the kind permission of their respective publishers:

E. E. CUMMINGS: Harcourt, Brace and Co., Inc., for "pity this busy monster, manunkind," "o by the by," and "what if a much of a which of a wind," copyright 1944 by E. E. Cummings; "the hours rise up," "a wind has blown," "in Just-," and "Buffalo Bill's," copyright 1923, 1951, by E. E. Cummings; "Spring is like a perhaps hand," copyright 1925 by E. E. Cummings; "my sweet old etcetera," copyright 1926 by Horace Liveright, renewed 1954 by E. E. Cummings; and "anyone lived in a pretty how town," copyright 1940 by E. E. Cummings. All reprinted from *Poems 1923-1954* by E. E. Cummings by permission of Harcourt, Brace and Co., Inc.

EMILY DICKINSON: The President and Fellows of Harvard College, for "Tell all the Truth" and "Because I could not stop for Death," from *The Poems of Emily Dickinson*, edited by Thomas H. Johnson, copyright 1951, 1955, by the President and Fellows of Harvard College. By permission of the Harvard University Press.
Little, Brown and Co., for "This quiet Dust," from *The Single Hound*, by Emily Dickinson, copyright 1914, 1922, by Martha Dickinson Bianchi. By permission of Little, Brown and Co.

ROBERT FROST: Holt, Rinehart and Winston, Inc., for nine poems from *You Come Too* by Robert Frost, copyright 1916, 1921, 1923, © 1959, by Henry Holt and Co., Inc., copyright 1936, 1942, 1944, 1951, by Robert Frost. By permission of Holt, Rinehart and Winston, Inc.

ROBINSON JEFFERS: Random House, Inc., for "Science," and "Boats in a Fog," copyright 1925 and renewed 1953 by Robinson Jeffers, and "To His Father," copyright 1924 and renewed 1951 by Robinson Jeffers, all reprinted from *Roan Stallion, Tamar, And Other Poems*, by Robinson Jeffers; "Rock and Hawk," copyright 1935 by the Modern Library, Inc., and "Tor House," and "Hurt Hawks," copyright 1928 and renewed 1956 by Robinson Jeffers, all reprinted from *The Selected Poetry of Robinson Jeffers*; "Battle (May 28, 1940)," copyright 1941 by Robinson Jeffers, reprinted from *Be Angry at the Sun and Other Poems*, by Robinson Jeffers; and "The Eye," copyright 1948 by Robinson Jeffers, reprinted from *The Double Axe and Other Poems*, by Robinson Jeffers. By permission of Random House, Inc.

ROBERT LOWELL: Harcourt, Brace and Co., Inc., for "The Exile's Return" and "The Quaker Graveyard in Nantucket," from *Lord Weary's Castle*, copyright 1944, 1946, by Robert Lowell; and "Mother Marie Therese," from *The Mills of the Kavanaughs*, copyright 1946, 1947, 1948, 1950, 1951, by Robert Lowell. Reprinted by permission of Harcourt, Brace and Co., Inc.

EZRA POUND: New Directions, for "The Seafarer," "A Pact," "In a Station of the Metro," "The River-Merchant's Wife: A Letter," and "E.P. Ode Pour L'Election de Son Sepulchre," all from *Personae, The Collected Poems of Ezra Pound*, copyright 1926 by Ezra Pound; and Canto II, from *The Cantos of Ezra Pound*, copyright 1934 by Ezra Pound. Reprinted by permission of New Directions.

EDWIN ARLINGTON ROBINSON: Charles Scribner's Sons, for "How Annandale Went Out" and "Miniver Cheevy," from *The Town Down the River*, by Edwin Arlington Robinson, copyright 1910 by Charles Scribner's Sons, 1938 by Ruth Nivison. Reprinted by permission of the publishers.
The Macmillan Company for "Flammonde," "The Dark Hills," "The Sheaves," and "Karma," copyright 1916 (R.1944), 1920 (R.1948), 1925 (R.1943) by The Macmillan Company; "Mr. Flood's Party" and "Many Are Called," copyright 1921 (R.1949) by Edwin Arlington Robinson, all from *Collected Poems of Edwin Arlington Robinson*, copyright 1935, 1937, by The Macmillan Company. Reprinted by permission of the publishers.

WALLACE STEVENS: Alfred A. Knopf, Inc., for six poems from *The Collected Poems of Wallace Stevens*, copyright 1923, 1931, 1935, 1936, 1942, 1954, by Wallace Stevens. Reprinted by permission of Alfred A Knopf, Inc.

WILLIAM CARLOS WILLIAMS: New Directions, for "Tract," "El Hombre," "To Waken an Old Lady," "The Widow's Lament in Springtime," "The Sea-Elephant," "The Yachts," and "The Term," all from *The Collected Earlier Poems of William Carlos Williams*, copyright 1938, 1951, by William Carlos Williams; and "The Dance," from *The Collected Later Poems of William Carlos Williams*, copyright 1944, 1948, and 1950, by William Carlos Williams. Reprinted by permission of New Directions.

# PREFACE

## TO THE AMERICAN EDITION

This little volume comes on the American market by an accident. It was originally designed to introduce American poetry to readers of English in Sweden. When we found it appealed to a number of new readers of American poetry in this country as well, we proposed to the Oxford University Press that it bring out an American edition. The result is in your hands.

Its special character follows from its origin. As an *introduction*, it had no need to be either comprehensive or unusual in its selections—though some of them are relatively unanthologized—but simply to present a limited number of well-known poems to an audience to whom they were not well known. On the other hand, being intended for mature and educated readers, it could reflect with little compromise the best modern taste, emphasizing recent rather than earlier poets and excluding the second-rate, however popular. In our own contributions to the book also we could avoid textbook condescension. The introductory notes on each poet are adult critical discussions with a certain interest of their own. Notes on individual poems are confined to the back where they will not obtrude on those who prefer their poetry unheckled. We also asked for and got a pleasant, uncrowded page which backs up our ruling principle that there is no hurry about poetry and no virtue in quantity, that one poem well read and made one's own is better than a dozen "covered" and forgotten.

Our book, we like to think, is in the tradition of Thoreau, Hawthorne, and Emily Dickinson rather than in that of Whitman, Dreiser, or Thomas Wolfe. Its motto is not, "I am vast, I contain multitudes," but "Simplify, simplify." It is designed in conscious opposition to the jumbo anthologies now in vogue, the "Treasuries," the "Libraries," both portable and complete with stand, with their rank on rank of closely printed verse. Instead, it tries to show the same respect for the single poem as do the volumes from which its selections are taken. To avoid the salesman's-sample-case effect of many small anthologies it makes a severe selection of poets as well as of poems. In the words of our original preface, "It concentrates on a limited number of representative poets from the time of Poe to the present in order to provide a selection from each one that will be adequate to convey the central fact about American poets, their vigorous individuality. All of them could have written, as one of them did, 'Whoso touches this book, touches a man.' We have tried here to put the reader in touch, not with a miscellaneous nationalistic blur, but with twelve men, or to speak accurately, eleven men and one woman. If in listening to these distinctive voices he comes to make the discovery that this branch of literature in English has produced some major poets whose work he will want to admit into the life of his own mind, the volume will have fulfilled all the hopes of its editors."

The problem of selection for such a book would of course have been excruciating if we had not early decided to relax about it. We concede without argument that as many poets as good or better are excluded as are included; that there is no magic in the number twelve; that each of the poets we do include has written scores of other poems we might just as well have chosen; that no one else doing the job would have done it as we have. This is, once more, an introduction, intended to give the reader a first glimpse of a world he has not explored and to start him on his way. The reader, if that is the name for him, who craves the assurance that after he has gotten through the poems in our volume he will *never have to read any more* will certainly not be happy with us, nor we with him.

A word might be said of one or two of our particular decisions. T. S. Eliot is not available for paperback anthologies and so had to be excluded. Otherwise, our American edition would certainly have become *Thirteen American Poets*. Our European readers did not miss him, as it would not occur to them that he could be thought an American. Most of Whitman's best-known poems are too long for our space. We believe, however, that this limitation has been a blessing in disguise, in that it has allowed us to concentrate on some of the small poems that are usually drowned out by his more operatic performances. Our Whitman is a bit unusual for an introductory anthology, but has a quality of his own which some might even prefer to the more expansive bard.

As for the choice of poets, we played this by ear too, trying only not to get an unbalanced or over-modish selection. To quote once more from our Swedish introduction: "The twelve representative American poets in this book fall, by accident rather than by design, into certain symmetries. The main division comes between the first and last six, the last being not just modern but modernist, writing under the full influence of the revolution in English verse which we associate with the names of Eliot and Pound and with the Imagist movement of the time of the First World War, while the first 'take off' from some older tradition and tend in some cases to respect tradition as such more than the second. Within the first group of six, the first three represent among them three main types of American poet: Longfellow, the skilful, conservative, predictable poet who provides the staple of the general verse-reading public; Poe, the deliberate craftsman, the 'poet's poet'; Whitman, the spontaneous bard. The second three, all from the same region of the country, are all essentially conservative poets whose creative power drove them into originality. The first three of our second six are dominant influences among modern American poets, exclusive of Eliot, whom Americans but not Europeans regard as American; the last three are strongly individual but less influential voices. Fortunately these symmetries are not perfect: Jeffers is hardly modernist, Lowell is in a class by himself, and all these poets are such individuals that to group them in any way is to violate their integrity."

All we would say by way of preface to our American readers can really be said very simply: Here are 100 good American poems. We hope you will enjoy them. There are plenty more where they came from.

STEPHEN WHICHER
LARS ÅHNEBRINK

*September* 1960

# CONTENTS

## VI. ROBERT FROST                                  83

## VII. WALLACE STEVENS                              98

# Twelve American Poets

# HENRY WADSWORTH LONGFELLOW

1807–1882

Frequent busloads of tourists stop every summer weekend outside of Craigie House on Brattle St. in Cambridge, Massachusetts, the home of Henry Wadsworth Longfellow. His name is still among the most familiar to the American reading public, both for certain "household" poems such as "The Psalm of Life," "The Village Blacksmith," and "Paul Revere's Ride," and for once widely read tales such as *Evangeline, Hiawatha,* or *The Courtship of Miles Standish.* He is the foremost among the so-called "schoolroom" poets of the last century—bearded, three-named bards of the middle classes such as William Cullen Bryant, James Russell Lowell, John Greenleaf Whittier, and Oliver Wendell Holmes (father of the jurist), whose portraits still dignify the walls of many school and college classrooms throughout the United States and whose poems appear in every anthology edited for Americans.

His life, like his poems, was on the whole easy and successful. On graduation from Bowdoin College in Maine, where he was a classmate of the novelist, Nathaniel Hawthorne, he was offered a professorship of modern languages there on condition that he first learn some. After three years of travel and study in Europe he returned to his professorship. Seven years later, after another briefer visit to Europe, he was made Smith Professor of French and Spanish at Harvard. In 1843 he married for the second time and moved into the handsome house, a gift from his wealthy father-in-law, that remained his home for the rest of his life. Though many

widely popular volumes of prose and verse came regularly
from his pen, he felt his professorship stifled his poetic
powers and in 1854 resigned his post to devote all his time
to literature. Personal tragedy struck in 1861, when his wife
was accidentally burned to death. His long religious closet
drama, or collection of dramas, *Christus,* and a translation
of Dante helped to combat his lasting grief. The sonnets he
wrote at this time are among his most highly regarded work.
Honors were heaped on him in his later years, among them
degrees from Oxford and Cambridge and a private audience
with the Queen, and after his death he became the only
American to be honored with a bust in the Poets' Corner
of Westminster Abbey.

His poems reflect the spirit of the romanticism of gentle
sentiment of his time, as distinguished from "high" or Gothic
romanticism. He belongs in the history of Western literature
with Burns, Campbell and Moore, Lamb and Goldsmith,
rather than with Byron or Shelley. His chief service to his
own time, like that of Washington Irving, was to introduce
something of the history-laden atmosphere of the Old World
to American readers and also to popularize American themes
abroad. Most modern critics are content to put him in a
class of writer familiar in every minor literature—the worthy,
competent author who is widely known in his own country
but is of little interest in any other. Unlike the other school-
room poets, however, it is not certain that he belongs there.
His themes were simple, certainly, his ideas unoriginal, his
forms and diction conventional (barring unfortunate aca-
demic experiments such as the use of the meter of the Finn-
ish *Kalevala* for *Hiawatha* or of Goethe's *Hermann und
Dorothea* for *Evangeline*); but he showed repeatedly, not
always in his most popular work, a control of tone, a skillful
blend of tact and humor with genuine feeling, which en-

titles him to serious respect. A nice rendering of the implied social occasion of the poem, an unusual, "social, urbane, highly cultivated, self-confident, temperate and easy" tone, to use the words of I. A. Richards, is conspicuous in such little-read lyrics as "The Fire of Drift-Wood" and "In the Churchyard at Cambridge," as well as in some of the longer tales. In such work there is nothing provincial or time-bound. Longfellow, like Gray, had the rare art to refresh the commonplace, and for this reason he will always hold a place in any well-selected collection of the best poems in the English language.

BIBLIOGRAPHY: Useful comment on Longfellow may be found in *Henry Wadsworth Longfellow; Representative Selections,* edited by Odell Shepard (New York, 1934), which includes an annotated bibliography; Lawrance Thompson, *Young Longfellow* (New York, 1938); George Arms, *The Fields Were Green* (Stanford, Calif., 1953), which includes a brief selection; and I. A. Richards, *Practical Criticism* (London, 1929). Selections in handy editions are the Modern Library (New York, 1945) and Dell (New York, 1959).

## *The Day Is Done*

THE day is done, and the darkness
    Falls from the wings of Night,
As a feather is wafted downward
    From an eagle in his flight.

I see the lights of the village
    Gleam through the rain and the mist,
And a feeling of sadness comes o'er me
    That my soul cannot resist:

A feeling of sadness and longing,
    That is not akin to pain,
And resembles sorrow only
    As the mist resembles the rain.

Come, read to me some poem,
    Some simple and heartfelt lay,
That shall soothe this restless feeling,
    And banish the thoughts of day.

Not from the grand old masters,
    Not from the bards sublime,
Whose distant footsteps echo
    Through the corridors of Time.

For, like strains of martial music,
    Their mighty thoughts suggest
Life's endless toil and endeavor;
    And to-night I long for rest.

Read from some humbler poet,
    Whose songs gushed from his heart,
As showers from the clouds of summer,
    Or tears from the eyelids start;

Who, through long days of labor,
    And nights devoid of ease,
Still heard in his soul the music
    Of wonderful melodies.

Such songs have power to quiet
    The restless pulse of care,
And come like the benediction
    That follows after prayer.

Then read from the treasured volume
    The poem of thy choice,
And lend to the rhyme of the poet
    The beauty of thy voice.

And the night shall be filled with music,
    And the cares, that infest the day,
Shall fold their tents, like the Arabs,
    And as silently steal away.

## Seaweed

WHEN descends on the Atlantic
    The gigantic
Storm-wind of the equinox,
Landward in his wrath he scourges
    The toiling surges,
Laden with seaweed from the rocks:

From Bermuda's reefs; from edges
    Of sunken ledges,
In some far-off, bright Azore;
From Bahama, and the dashing,
    Silver-flashing
Surges of San Salvador;

From the tumbling surf, that buries
    The Orkneyan skerries,
Answering the hoarse Hebrides;
And from wrecks of ships, and drifting
    Spars, uplifting
On the desolate, rainy seas;—

Ever drifting, drifting, drifting
    On the shifting
Currents of the restless main;
Till in sheltered coves, and reaches
    Of sandy beaches,
All have found repose again.

So when storms of wild emotion
    Strike the ocean
Of the poet's soul, erelong
From each cave and rocky fastness,
    In its vastness,
Floats some fragment of a song:

From the far-off isles enchanted,
    Heaven has planted
With the golden fruit of Truth;
From the flashing surf, whose vision
    Gleams Elysian
In the tropic clime of Youth;

From the strong Will, and the Endeavor
    That forever
Wrestle with the tides of Fate;
From the wreck of Hopes far-scattered,
    Tempest-shattered,
Floating waste and desolate;—

Ever drifting, drifting, drifting
    On the shifting
Currents of the restless heart;
Till at length in books recorded,
    They, like hoarded
Household words, no more depart.


## The Fire of Drift-Wood

### Devereux Farm, near Marblehead

WE sat within the farm-house old,
    Whose windows, looking o'er the bay,
Gave to the sea-breeze damp and cold
    An easy entrance, night and day.

Not far away we saw the port,
    The strange, old-fashioned, silent town,
The lighthouse, the dismantled fort,
    The wooden houses, quaint and brown.

We sat and talked until the night,
    Descending, filled the little room;
Our faces faded from the sight,
    Our voices only broke the gloom.

We spake of many a vanished scene,
    Of what we once had thought and said,
Of what had been, and might have been,
    And who was changed, and who was dead;

And all that fills the hearts of friends,
    When first they feel, with secret pain,
Their lives henceforth have separate ends,
    And never can be one again;

The first slight swerving of the heart,
    That words are powerless to express,
And leave it still unsaid in part,
    Or say it in too great excess.

The very tones in which we spake
    Had something strange, I could but mark;
The leaves of memory seemed to make
    A mournful rustling in the dark.

Oft died the words upon our lips,
    As suddenly, from out the fire
Built of the wreck of stranded ships,
    The flames would leap and then expire.

And, as their splendor flashed and failed,
    We thought of wrecks upon the main,
Of ships dismasted, that were hailed
    And sent no answer back again.

The windows, rattling in their frames,
    The ocean, roaring up the beach,
The gusty blast, the bickering flames,
    All mingled vaguely in our speech;

Until they made themselves a part
    Of fancies floating through the brain,
The long-lost ventures of the heart,
    That send no answers back again.

O flames that glowed! O hearts that yearned!
    They were indeed too much akin,
The drift-wood fire without that burned,
    The thoughts that burned and glowed within.

## In the Churchyard at Cambridge

In the village churchyard she lies,
Dust is in her beautiful eyes,
    No more she breathes, nor feels, nor stirs;
At her feet and at her head
Lies a slave to attend the dead,
    But their dust is white as hers.

Was she, a lady of high degree,
So much in love with the vanity
    And foolish pomp of this world of ours?
Or was it Christian charity,
And lowliness and humility,
    The richest and rarest of all dowers?

Who shall tell us? No one speaks;
No color shoots into those cheeks,
    Either of anger or of pride,
At the rude question we have asked;
Nor will the mystery be unmasked
    By those who are sleeping at her side.

Hereafter?—And do you think to look
On the terrible pages of that Book
    To find her failings, faults, and errors?
Ah, you will then have other cares,
In your own shortcomings and despairs,
    In your own secret sins and terrors!

## Chaucer

An old man in a lodge within a park;
    The chamber walls depicted all around
    With portraitures of huntsman, hawk, and hound,
    And the hurt deer. He listeneth to the lark,

Whose song comes with the sunshine through the dark
　　Of painted glass in leaden lattice bound;
　　He listeneth and he laugheth at the sound,
　　Then writeth in a book like any clerk.
He is the poet of the dawn, who wrote
　　The Canterbury Tales, and his old age
　　Made beautiful with song; and as I read
I hear the crowing cock, I hear the note
　　Of lark and linnet, and from every page
　　Rise odors of ploughed field or flowery mead.


## The Cross of Snow

In the long, sleepless watches of the night,
　　A gentle face—the face of one long dead—
　　Looks at me from the wall, where round its head
　　The night-lamp casts a halo of pale light.
Here in this room she died; and soul more white
　　Never through martyrdom of fire was led
　　To its repose; nor can in books be read
　　The legend of a life more benedight.
There is a mountain in the distant West
　　That, sun-defying, in its deep ravines
　　Displays a cross of snow upon its side.
Such is the cross I wear upon my breast
　　These eighteen years, through all the changing scenes
　　And seasons, changeless since the day she died.

# EDGAR ALLAN POE

## 1809–1849

Edgar Allan Poe, like Falstaff, was not only an inventor but a cause that invention was in other men. His aloof and touchy personality made him many enemies who invented after his death a morbid, corrupt and dissolute figure, the embodiment of all the Philistine's worst suspicions of the artist. Not long after, Baudelaire and his Symbolist successors invented *Edgarpo*, "the tragic young aristocrat, alone in a barbarous, gaslit America," as Marcus Cunliffe paraphrases it, forerunner of the *poète maudit*. In truth, Poe was neither of these. His own life, as Edward Davidson writes, was "one of the dullest any figure of literary importance has lived in the past two hundred years" (perhaps a slight overstatement). No undisciplined person could have accomplished so much highly disciplined work. He was not a user of drugs, not even a drunkard in any ordinary sense (one drink of any alcoholic beverage made him "a madman," and his own sufferings, along with the convivial habits of his times, made it sometimes impossible for him to refuse that drink). His relationship to women, while distastefully perfervid, was entirely honorable and chivalrous, not to say innocent. The legend of the corrupt Poe has persisted because it seems to fit his writings. But, as Davidson puts it, "Poe wrote what he did because it was as remote as possible from his own experience."

As for the "aristocrat," the undeniable gap between Poe and his fellows was not so much that of the genius and the multitude as that of the showman and his audience. Poe, like Shaw, was a *histrio,* a man whose essence, if he had any, lay undiscoverable behind a succession of masks. There are many Poes. He was a skillful professional editor of magazines; a shrewd manufacturer of first-class articles for the literary market-place; an idealistic and fastidious literary craftsman; a pioneer explorer of the depths of the subrational mind; an icily keen intellect, cutting to the heart of problems with the scalpel of logic, like the detective in his murder mysteries; an unremitting if sometimes captious campaigner for high critical standards; a provocative if narrow aesthetic theorist; a hypnotic if limited poet; and withal he had something of the dazzle of genius about him too.

His life demonstrates the old truth that there is nothing romantic about poverty, being one long and nearly unavailing struggle for the means to live. The orphan son of itinerant actors, he was brought up in the home of a wealthy merchant in Richmond, Virginia, but became estranged from his foster father as he grew older, until at the age of twenty-two he found himself cast out on the world to live by his own efforts. The story of his life thereafter is a chronicle of editorial positions on various literary magazines in Baltimore, Philadelphia, and New York and of steady publication in prose and verse, activities which won him considerable reputation but no economic security. His own emotional instability, poor judgment of men, and talent for making enemies insured his failure; his pride, sensitivity, and lack of humor magnified his suffering. His private life was pitiful also, as his child-wife, Virginia Clemm, died after years of hardship and illness which drove him nearly mad. Though his own death a few years later was somewhat mysterious (he was found delirious in the streets of Baltimore and died four days later) his increasing melancholy and instability made some such end almost inevitable.

The bulk of Poe's poems were written in his youth, though he revised them ceaselessly throughout his life. His poetic themes and style were established early and changed little. Characteristically, he worked out an elaborate rationale of what he was doing, somewhat after the fact, in his poetic theory, as presented in his late essay, "The Poetic Principle." He held that the only effect proper to poetry was to stir the "poetic sentiment," a sense of "supernal Loveliness" felt through and beyond earthly beauty. He therefore on the one hand rejected "the Didactic" in poetry, meaning any concern with intellectual or especially with moral truth, and on the other stressed the analogy of poetry and music, since the awareness poetry should stir was ultimately ineffable. It followed logically also that, if a poem succeeds only as it excites, it cannot succeed if its reading is interrupted: hence "a long poem does not exist." Although the theory, compounded of Coleridge and romantic Platonism, carries the self-refutation of most products of ingenious logic, it fits Poe's practice well, since in his poems the rational subject counts for little while the indefinite suggestions of the words in their arrangement constitute the poem.

Criticism has never agreed as to Poe's success. One may point to his rather obvious conception of "music" in verse—cloyingly mellifluous sounds, a "walloping meter," elaborate stanzas and refrains, etc.—, to his inaccurate and unremarkable use of words, to the frequent banality of his content, and to the quality of theatrical trickery that clings to all Poe's work, as evidence of a rather vulgar second-rateness. Or one may point out that all these defects may be easily exaggerated and that in any case they are the defects of qualities necessary to Poe's special hypnotic purpose; that there may be more to his subject-matter than meets the supercilious eye; and that his theory and practice have had such a lasting influence on modern verse that the burden of proof lies on the detractor, not the defender. The ordinary reader, therefore, is fortunately thrown into the position he abandons too easily with "classic" authors, that of judging for himself, and an impressive number of ordinary readers continue to give a favorable verdict on Poe.

BIBLIOGRAPHY: The best edition of Poe's poems and one of the finest critical editions of any American author is *The Poems of Edgar Allan Poe,* edited by Killis Campbell (Boston, 1917). Professor Campbell's many articles on Poe are still useful; a representative group of studies are collected in *The Mind of Poe and Other Studies* (Cambridge, Mass., 1933). The most authoritative recent life is Arthur Hobson Quinn, *Edgar Allan Poe* (New York, 1941); the older life by George Woodberry is still valuable for critical insights, as is Edward H. Davidson, *Poe: A Critical Study* (Cambridge, Mass., 1957). His *Selected Writings of Edgar Allan Poe* (Boston, 1956) is handy and reasonable in price as is the Dell *Complete Poems* (New York, 1959).

## The City in the Sea

Lo! Death has reared himself a throne
In a strange city lying alone
Far down within the dim West,
Where the good and the bad and the worst and the best
Have gone to their eternal rest.
There shrines and palaces and towers
(Time-eaten towers that tremble not!)
Resemble nothing that is ours.
Around, by lifting winds forgot,
Resignedly beneath the sky
The melancholy waters lie.

No rays from the holy heaven come down
On the long night-time of that town;
But light from out the lurid sea
Streams up the turrets silently—
Gleams up the pinnacles far and free—
Up domes—up spires—up kingly halls—

Up fanes—up Babylon-like walls—
Up shadowy long-forgotten bowers
Of sculptured ivy and stone flowers—
Up many and many a marvellous shrine
Whose wreathèd friezes intertwine
The viol, the violet, and the vine.

Resignedly beneath the sky
The melancholy waters lie.
So blend the turrets and shadows there
That all seem pendulous in air,
While from a proud tower in the town
Death looks gigantically down.

There open fanes and gaping graves
Yawn level with the luminous waves;
But not the riches there that lie
In each idol's diamond eye—
Not the gaily-jewelled dead
Tempt the waters from their bed;
For no ripples curl, alas!
Along that wilderness of glass—
No swellings tell that winds may be
Upon some far-off happier sea—
No heavings hint that winds have been
On seas less hideously serene.

But lo, a stir is in the air!
The wave—there is a movement there!
As if the towers had thrust aside,
In slightly sinking, the dull tide—
As if their tops had feebly given
A void within the filmy Heaven.
The waves have now a redder glow—
The hours are breathing faint and low—
And when, amid no earthly moans,
Down, down that town shall settle hence,
Hell, rising from a thousand thrones,
Shall do it reverence.

## The Raven

ONCE upon a midnight dreary, while I pondered, weak and
    weary,
Over many a quaint and curious volume of forgotten lore—
While I nodded, nearly napping, suddenly there came a
    tapping, .

As of some one gently rapping, rapping at my chamber door.
' 'T is some visitor,' I muttered, 'tapping at my chamber
   door—
                Only this and nothing more.'

Ah, distinctly I remember it was in the bleak December;
And each separate dying ember wrought its ghost upon the
   floor.
Eagerly I wished the morrow;—vainly I had sought to
   borrow
From my books surcease of sorrow—sorrow for the lost
   Lenore—
For the rare and radiant maiden whom the angels name
   Lenore—
                Nameless *here* for evermore.

And the silken, sad, uncertain rustling of each purple
   curtain
Thrilled me—filled me with fantastic terrors never felt
   before;
So that now, to still the beating of my heart, I stood
   repeating,
' 'T is some visitor entreating entrance at my chamber
   door—
Some late visitor entreating entrance at my chamber door;—
                This it is and nothing more.'

Presently my soul grew stronger; hesitating then no longer,
'Sir,' said I, 'or Madam, truly your forgiveness I implore;
But the fact is I was napping, and so gently you came
   rapping,
And so faintly you came tapping, tapping at my chamber
   door,
That I scarce was sure I heard you'—here I opened wide
   the door;—
                Darkness there and nothing more.

Deep into that darkness peering, long I stood there won-
    dering, fearing,
Doubting, dreaming dreams no mortal ever dared to dream
    before;
But the silence was unbroken, and the stillness gave no
    token,
And the only word there spoken was the whispered word,
    'Lenore?'
This I whispered, and an echo murmured back the word,
    'Lenore!'
            Merely this and nothing more.

Back into the chamber turning, all my soul within me
    burning,
Soon again I heard a tapping somewhat louder than before.
'Surely,' said I, 'surely that is something at my window
    lattice;
Let me see, then, what thereat is, and this mystery explore—
Let my heart be still a moment and this mystery explore;—
        'T is the wind and nothing more!'

Open here I flung the shutter, when, with many a flirt and
    flutter,
In there stepped a stately Raven of the saintly days of yore;
Not the least obeisance made he; not a minute stopped or
    stayed he;
But, with mien of lord or lady, perched above my chamber
    door—
Perched upon a bust of Pallas just above my chamber
    door—
        Perched, and sat, and nothing more.

Then this ebony bird beguiling my sad fancy into smiling,
By the grave and stern decorum of the countenance it wore,
'Though thy crest be shorn and shaven, thou,' I said, 'art
    sure no craven,

Ghastly grim and ancient Raven wandering from the Nightly
    shore—
Tell me what thy lordly name is on the Night's Plutonian
    shore!'
           Quoth the Raven, 'Nevermore.'

Much I marvelled this ungainly fowl to hear discourse so
    plainly,
Though its answer little meaning—little relevancy bore;
For we cannot help agreeing that no living human being
Ever yet was blessed with seeing bird above his chamber
    door—
Bird or beast upon the sculptured bust above his chamber
    door,
          With such name as 'Nevermore.'

But the Raven, sitting lonely on the placid bust, spoke only
That one word, as if his soul in that one word he did
    outpour.
Nothing farther then he uttered—not a feather then he
    fluttered—
Till I scarcely more than muttered, 'Other friends have
    flown before—
On the morrow *he* will leave me, as my Hopes have flown
    before.'
          Then the bird said, 'Nevermore.'

Startled at the stillness broken by reply so aptly spoken,
'Doubtless,' said I, 'what it utters is its only stock and store
Caught from some unhappy master whom unmerciful
    Disaster
Followed fast and followed faster till his songs one burden
    bore—
Till the dirges of his Hope that melancholy burden bore
          Of "Never—nevermore." '

But the Raven still beguiling my sad fancy into smiling,
Straight I wheeled a cushioned seat in front of bird and
    bust and door;
Then, upon the velvet sinking, I betook myself to linking
Fancy unto fancy, thinking what this ominous bird of yore—
What this grim, ungainly, ghastly, gaunt, and ominous bird
    of yore
        Meant in croaking 'Nevermore.'

This I sat engaged in guessing, but no syllable expressing
To the fowl whose fiery eyes now burned into my bosom's
    core;
This and more I sat divining, with my head at ease reclining
On the cushion's velvet lining that the lamp-light gloated
    o'er,
But whose velvet-violet lining with the lamp-light gloating
    o'er,
        *She* shall press, ah, nevermore!

Then, methought, the air grew denser, perfumed from an
    unseen censer
Swung by seraphim whose foot-falls tinkled on the tufted
    floor.
'Wretch,' I cried, 'thy God hath lent thee—by these angels
    he hath sent thee
Respite—respite and nepenthe from thy memories of Lenore;
Quaff, oh, quaff this kind nepenthe and forget this lost
    Lenore!'
        Quoth the Raven, 'Nevermore.'

'Prophet!' said I, 'thing of evil!—prophet still, if bird or
    devil!—
Whether Tempter sent, or whether tempest tossed thee here
    ashore,

Desolate yet all undaunted, on this desert land enchanted—
On this home by Horror haunted—tell me truly, I implore—
Is there—*is* there balm in Gilead?—tell me—tell me, I
implore!'
　　　　　Quoth the Raven, 'Nevermore.'

'Prophet!' said I, 'thing of evil!—prophet still, if bird or
devil!
By that Heaven that bends above us—by that God we both
adore—
Tell this soul with sorrow laden if, within the distant
Aidenn,
It shall clasp a sainted maiden whom the angels name
Lenore—
Clasp a rare and radiant maiden whom the angels name
Lenore.'
　　　　　Quoth the Raven, 'Nevermore.'

'Be that word our sign of parting, bird or fiend!' I shrieked,
upstarting—
'Get thee back into the tempest and the Night's Plutonian
shore!
Leave no black plume as a token of that lie thy soul hath
spoken!
Leave my loneliness unbroken!—quit the bust above my
door!
Take thy beak from out my heart, and take thy form from
off my door!'
　　　　　Quoth the Raven, 'Nevermore.'

And the Raven, never flitting, still is sitting, *still* is sitting
On the pallid bust of Pallas just above my chamber door;
And his eyes have all the seeming of a demon's that is
dreaming,

And the lamp-light o'er him streaming throws his shadow
    on the floor;
And my soul from out that shadow that lies floating on the
    floor
        Shall be lifted—nevermore!


## Ulalume—A Ballad

THE skies they were ashen and sober;
    The leaves they were crispéd and sere—
    The leaves they were withering and sere:
It was night, in the lonesome October
    Of my most immemorial year:
It was hard by the dim lake of Auber,
    In the misty mid region of Weir—
It was down by the dank tarn of Auber,
    In the ghoul-haunted woodland of Weir.


Here once, through an alley Titanic,
    Of cypress, I roamed with my Soul—
    Of cypress, with Psyche, my Soul.
These were days when my heart was volcanic
    As the scoriac rivers that roll—
    As the lavas that restlessly roll
Their sulphurous currents down Yaanek
    In the ultimate climes of the Pole—
That groan as they roll down Mount Yaanek
    In the realms of the Boreal Pole.


Our talk had been serious and sober,
    But our thoughts they were palsied and sere—
    Our memories were treacherous and sere;

For we knew not the month was October,
    And we marked not the night of the year
    (Ah, night of all nights in the year!)—
We noted not the dim lake of Auber
    (Though once we had journeyed down here)—
We remembered not the dank tarn of Auber,
    Nor the ghoul-haunted woodland of Weir.

And now, as the night was senescent
    And star-dials pointed to morn—
    As the star-dials hinted of morn—
At the end of our path a liquescent
    And nebulous lustre was born,
Out of which a miraculous crescent
    Arose with a duplicate horn—
Astarte's bediamonded crescent
    Distinct with its duplicate horn.

And I said: 'She is warmer than Dian;
    She rolls through an ether of sighs—
    She revels in a region of sighs.
She has seen that the tears are not dry on
    These cheeks, where the worm never dies,
And has come past the stars of the Lion,
    To point us the path to the skies—
    To the Lethean peace of the skies—
Come up, in despite of the Lion,
    To shine on us with her bright eyes—
Come up through the lair of the Lion,
    With love in her luminous eyes.'

But Psyche, uplifting her finger,
    Said: 'Sadly this star I mistrust—
    Her pallor I strangely mistrust:

Ah, hasten!—ah, let us not linger!
　　Ah, fly!—let us fly!—for we must.'
In terror she spoke, letting sink her
　　Wings till they trailed in the dust—
In agony sobbed, letting sink her
　　Plumes till they trailed in the dust—
　　Till they sorrowfully trailed in the dust.

I replied: 'This is nothing but dreaming:
　　Let us on by this tremulous light!
　　Let us bathe in this crystalline light!
Its Sibyllic splendor is beaming
　　With Hope and in Beauty to-night:—
　　See!—it flickers up the sky through the night!
Ah, we safely may trust to its gleaming,
　　And be sure it will lead us aright—
We surely may trust to a gleaming,
　　That cannot but guide us aright,
　　Since it flickers up to Heaven through the night.'

Thus I pacified Psyche and kissed her,
　　And tempted her out of her gloom—
　　And conquered her scruples and gloom;
And we passed to the end of the vista,
　　But were stopped by the door of a tomb—
　　By the door of a legended tomb;
And I said: 'What is written, sweet sister,
　　On the door of this legended tomb?'
　　She replied: 'Ulalume—Ulalume!—
　　'T is the vault of thy lost Ulalume!'

Then my heart it grew ashen and sober
　　As the leaves that were crispéd and sere—
　　As the leaves that were withering and sere;

And I cried: 'It was surely October
  On *this* very night of last year
  That I journeyed—I journeyed down here!—
  That I brought a dread burden down here—
  On this night of all nights in the year,
  Ah, what demon hath tempted me here?
Well I know, now, this dim lake of Auber—
  This misty mid region of Weir—
Well I know, now, this dank tarn of Auber,
  This ghoul-haunted woodland of Weir.'


Said we, then—the two, then: 'Ah, can it
  Have been that the woodlandish ghouls—
  The pitiful, the merciful ghouls—
To bar up our way and to ban it
  From the secret that lies in these wolds—
  From the thing that lies hidden in these wolds—
Have drawn up the spectre of a planet
  From the limbo of lunary souls—
This sinfully scintillant planet
  From the Hell of the planetary souls?'

# WALT WHITMAN

1819–1892

As with Poe, there is a Whitman legend which we have at last succeeded in putting aside to reveal a much more interesting if less "cosmic" figure. His legend has been harder to penetrate than Poe's, since it is a single, consistent one which he sedulously labored to create himself. The figure he wished to present to the world was a grand one: a prophet-priest of individualism, the religion of the modern; of democracy, the social order appropriate to it; and of the New World where the new order was coming to birth. The gigantic personality he projected was to be rival and successor of all previous religious prophets, including Christ; the archetypal poet of America as Virgil had been of Rome, Dante of medieval Europe, Shakespeare of Elizabethan England, or Goethe of modern Europe; the representative and ideal of the new democratic man. His startling poems, especially the early ones, sketched the portrait of this hero and "ventriloquized" for him with such infectious *élan* that he has repeatedly caught the imagination of democratic leaders in every land and has become, as his creator hoped, a type-figure of the democratic dream.

The trouble with larger-than-life postures like this is that they provoke a reaction. Whitman's has had its inevitable result in indignant exposés of his "pose," sharp satires from skeptics here and abroad, a flood of parodies, and a widespread tendency in recent times to write him off as an inflated reputation who not merely has little to say to us as a prophet but who was not even any great shakes as a poet.

WALT WHITMAN · 43

All this is a pity, for Whitman in fact is of absorbing interest as a poet and person. The first step to a just understanding of him is to see his poetic personality as a dramatic creation, a detached and magnified segment of his creator like many figures in avowed fiction (Ibsen's Brand, Melville's Ahab, Byron's Manfred come to mind), an ego-ideal who may be as much a compensation for deficiencies in his creator as a fulfillment of possibilities. Only then can we begin to make sense of the contrast between the passive, drifting, lounging Brooklyn journalist, wholly undistinguished in background and education, which was Whitman until the age of thirty-six, a man whose published and unpublished work show hardly the slightest sign of literary genius; and the astonishingly original and powerful voice which spoke up full volume in the first edition of *Leaves of Grass*, published in that year, and did not cease till death. In the great "Myself" that controls the imagined world of his poems Whitman found a release and fulfillment that he had never had and could not have in actual life.

The vision that inspired Whitman's poetic self, a recognizable variety of the mystical insight, is the infinite worth of reality simply as reality, a worth underlying and erasing all the value distinctions we are led to make by our position as animals struggling for survival. Unlike traditional mystics, however, unlike even the man he styled "Master," Ralph Waldo Emerson, he did not experience his reality as a "light that never was on sea or land," a supernal opposite to the physical world, but identified it completely with the world of actual things. He announced, not another world, but a new insight into the ordinary world, one which revealed the equal divinity of all men and all things and of every natural function. In his earlier and most oracular poems he carried his vision with superb daring to its logical conclusion and not only brushed aside all social distinctions and taboos, to become the poet of "many long dumb voices," but also affirmed a natural immortality and denied death. These ringing denials, in themselves foolish, opened the way to some of his best poems, as his sense of fact worked in vital dialectic with his faith to produce some of the most haunting meditations on death and evil in the language, notably his great elegy for Lincoln, "When Lilacs Last in the Dooryard Bloom'd."

The influence of Whitman's verse on Western literature, though less than Poe's, has been in the same direction. Two main characteristics of modern poetry, as singled out in a recent essay by Cleanth Brooks and Robert Penn Warren, that it is a "dramatic construct" and that it "forms a psychological, not a logical, unity," are both conspicuous in Whitman's verse. He also, like Poe, is a forerunner of Symbolism, though Symbolists and Imagists have been at pains to deny it. Unlike Poe, the form he evolved was the organic or "natural" poem that discarded traditional rhyme and meter for long irregular lines, distinguished from prose by their strong chanting rhythm and often arranged in long parallel series to resemble Whitman's favorite analogy for them, the successive breakers of the sea on a beach. Yet his aim was also, like Poe's, a kind of hypnosis, in this case of himself. Through such a form, both regular and free, he could "permit to speak at every hazard"; it allowed him to bring what we would now call the subconscious to expression. The result, even when formless (and it always has a *direction* if not a form), is a fascinating and often most evocative coalescence of buried associations, like the "image clusters" in Shakespeare's tragedies, which forms at its best an impressively rich and complex "psychological unity."

Unfortunately readers of this anthology will have to take

these statements largely on faith, since the poems that best illustrate them—"The Sleepers," "Song of Myself," "Crossing Brooklyn Ferry," "Out of the Cradle," "When Lilacs Last," etc.—are all too long to be included here. The poems we have chosen seem to us among the best of Whitman's *shorter* poems. Yet even here the dramatic quality is well illustrated in "A Sight in Camp" or "Whoever You Are," while the apparently aimless but actually subtly ordered and evocative series of images is represented in "There Was a Child." The more carefully and discriminatingly we read Whitman, the more reason we can find to think that his full recognition as a poet and an influence has not yet arrived.

BIBLIOGRAPHY: Instead of publishing a series of volumes, Whitman kept reissuing the first one, though the final edition of *Leaves of Grass* bears little resemblance to the first. He not only wrote hundreds of additional poems but constantly revised and rearranged the earlier ones. The first edition has been re-edited by Malcolm Cowley (New York, 1959). Other important editions are the third (1860), the fifth (1872), and the last (1891–92).

The best introduction to Whitman is Gay Wilson Allen's *Walt Whitman Handbook* (Chicago, 1946) and the authoritative account of Whitman's life is his *The Solitary Singer* (New York, 1955). The exploration of Whitman's inner life, as seen through the poems, including the question of his homoerotic tendencies, has been chiefly conducted by European scholars, among whom are Jean Catel, *Walt Whitman: La naissance du poète* (Paris, 1929), Frederik Schyberg, *Walt Whitman* (translated, New York, 1951), and Roger Asselineau, *L'Evolution de Walt Whitman* (Paris, 1954). A stimulating recent study is Richard Chase, *Walt Whitman Reconsidered* (New York, 1955). A useful critical aid is *Walt Whitman's Poems,* edited by Gay Wilson Allen and Charles T. Davis (New York University, 1955; Evergreen Books, 1959).

## One's-Self I Sing

ONE'S-SELF I sing, a simple separate person,
Yet utter the word Democratic, the word En-Masse.

Of physiology from top to toe I sing,
Not physiognomy alone nor brain alone is worthy for the
    Muse, I say the Form complete is worthier far,
The Female equally with the Male I sing.

Of Life immense in passion, pulse, and power,
Cheerful, for freest action form'd under the laws divine,
The Modern Man I sing.

## The Ship Starting

LO, the unbounded sea,
On its breast a ship starting, spreading all sails, carrying
    even her moonsails,
The pennant is flying aloft as she speeds she speeds so stately
    —below emulous waves press forward,
They surround the ship with shining curving motions and
    foam.

## There Was a Child Went Forth

THERE was a child went forth every day,
And the first object he look'd upon, that object he became,
And that object became part of him for the day or a certain
    part of the day,
Or for many years or stretching cycles of years.

The early lilacs became part of this child,
And grass and white and red morning-glories, and white
    and red clover, and the song of the phœbe-bird,

And the Third-month lambs and the sow's pink-faint litter,
    and the mare's foal and the cow's calf,
And the noisy brood of the barnyard or by the mire of the
    pond-side,
And the fish suspending themselves so curiously below there,
    and the beautiful curious liquid,
And the water-plants with their graceful flat heads, all
    became part of him.


The field-sprouts of Fourth-month and Fifth-month became
    part of him,
Winter-grain sprouts and those of the light-yellow corn,
    and the esculent roots of the garden,
And the apple-trees cover'd with blossoms and the fruit
    afterward, and wood-berries, and the commonest weeds
    by the road,
And the old drunkard staggering home from the outhouse
    of the tavern whence he had lately risen,
And the schoolmistress that pass'd on her way to the school,
And the friendly boys that pass'd, and the quarrelsome
    boys,
And the tidy and fresh-cheek'd girls, and the barefoot negro
    boy and girl,
And all the changes of city and country wherever he went.


His own parents, he that had father'd him and she that had
    conceiv'd him in her womb and birth'd him,
They gave this child more of themselves than that,
They gave him afterward every day, they became part of
    him.


The mother at home quietly placing the dishes on the
    supper-table,

The mother with mild words, clean her cap and gown, a wholesome odor falling off her person and clothes as she walks by,

The father, strong, self-sufficient, manly, mean, anger'd, unjust,

The blow, the quick loud word, the tight bargain, the crafty lure,

The family usages, the language, the company, the furniture, the yearning and swelling heart,

Affection that will not be gainsay'd, the sense of what is real, the thought if after all it should prove unreal,

The doubts of day-time and the doubts of night-time, the curious whether and how,

Whether that which appears so is so, or is it all flashes and specks?

Men and women crowding fast in the streets, if they are not flashes and specks what are they?

The streets themselves and the façades of houses, and goods in the windows,

Vehicles, teams, the heavy-plank'd wharves, the huge crossing at the ferries,

The village on the highland seen from afar at sunset, the river between,

Shadows, aureola and mist, the light falling on roofs and gables of white or brown two miles off,

The schooner near by sleepily dropping down the tide, the little boat slack-tow'd astern,

The hurrying tumbling waves, quick-broken crests, slapping,

The strata of color'd clouds, the long bar of maroon-tint away solitary by itself, the spread of purity it lies motionless in,

The horizon's edge, the flying sea-crow, the fragrance of salt marsh and shore mud,

These became part of that child who went forth every day,
and who now goes, and will always go forth every day.

## I Saw in Louisiana a Live-Oak Growing

I SAW in Louisiana a live-oak growing,
All alone stood it and the moss hung down from the branches,
Without any companion it grew there uttering joyous leaves
of dark green,
And its look, rude, unbending, lusty, made me think of
myself,
But I wonder'd how it could utter joyous leaves standing
alone there without its friend near, for I knew I could
not,
And I broke off a twig with a certain number of leaves
upon it, and twined around it a little moss,
And brought it away, and I have placed it in sight, in my
room,
It is not needed to remind me as of my own dear friends,
(For I believe lately I think of little else than of them,)
Yet it remains to me a curious token, it makes me think of
manly love;
For all that, and though the live-oak glistens there in
Louisiana solitary in a wide flat space,
Uttering joyous leaves all its life without a friend a lover
near,
I know very well I could not.

## Whoever You Are Holding Me Now in Hand

WHOEVER you are holding me now in hand,
Without one thing all will be useless,
I give you fair warning before you attempt me further,
I am not what you supposed, but far different.

Who is he that would become my follower?
Who would sign himself a candidate for my affections?

The way is suspicious, the result uncertain, perhaps destruc-
    tive,
You would have to give up all else, I alone would expect to
    be your sole and exclusive standard,
Your novitiate would even then be long and exhausting,
The whole past theory of your life and all conformity to the
    lives around you would have to be abandon'd,
Therefore release me now before troubling yourself any
    further, let go your hand from my shoulders,
Put me down and depart on your way.

Or else by stealth in some wood for trial,
Or back of a rock in the open air,
(For in any roof'd room of a house I emerge not, nor in
    company,
And in libraries I lie as one dumb, a gawk, or unborn, or
    dead,)
But just possibly with you on a high hill, first watching lest
    any person for miles around approach unawares,
Or possibly with you sailing at sea, or on the beach of the
    sea or some quiet island,
Here to put your lips upon mine I permit you,
With the comrade's long-dwelling kiss or the new husband's
    kiss,
For I am the new husband and I am the comrade.

Or if you will, thrusting me beneath your clothing,
Where I may feel the throbs of your heart or rest upon
    your hip,
Carry me when you go forth over land or sea;
For thus merely touching you is enough, is best,

And thus touching you would I silently sleep and be carried
    eternally.

But these leaves conning you con at peril,
For these leaves and me you will not understand,
They will elude you at first and still more afterward, I will
    certainly elude you,
Even while you should think you had unquestionably caught
    me, behold!
Already you see I have escaped from you.

For it is not for what I have put into it that I have written
    this book,
Nor is it by reading it you will acquire it,
Nor do those know me best who admire me and vauntingly
    praise me,
Nor will the candidates for my love (unless at most a very
    few) prove victorious,
Nor will my poems do good only, they will do just as much
    evil, perhaps more,
For all is useless without that which you may guess at many
    times and not hit, that which I hinted at;
Therefore release me and depart on your way.

## I Sit and Look Out

I sit and look out upon all the sorrows of the world, and
    upon all oppression and shame,
I hear secret convulsive sobs from young men at anguish
    with themselves, remorseful after deeds done,
I see in low life the mother misused by her children, dying,
    neglected, gaunt, desperate,

I see the wife misused by her husband, I see the treacherous
    seducer of young women,
I mark the ranklings of jealousy and unrequited love at-
    tempted to be hid, I see these sights on the earth,
I see the working of battle, pestilence, tyranny, I see martyrs
    and prisoners,
I observe a famine at sea, I observe the sailors casting lots
    who shall be kill'd to preserve the lives of the rest,
I observe the slights and degradations cast by arrogant per-
    sons upon laborers, the poor, and upon negroes, and
    the like;
All these—all the meanness and agony without end I sitting
    look out upon,
See, hear, and am silent.

## By the Bivouac's Fitful Flame

By the bivouac's fitful flame,
A procession winding around me, solemn and sweet and
    slow—but first I note,
The tents of the sleeping army, the fields' and woods' dim
    outline,
The darkness lit by spots of kindled fire, the silence,
Like a phantom far or near an occasional figure moving,
The shrubs and trees, (as I lift my eyes they seem to be
    stealthily watching me,)
While wind in procession thoughts, O tender and wondrous
    thoughts,
Of life and death, of home and the past and loved, and
    of those that are far away;
A solemn and slow procession there as I sit on the ground,
By the bivouac's fitful flame.

## A Sight in Camp in the Daybreak Gray and Dim

A SIGHT in camp in the daybreak gray and dim,
As from my tent I emerge so early sleepless,
As slow I walk in the cool fresh air the path near by the
    hospital tent,
Three forms I see on stretchers lying, brought out there
    untended lying,
Over each the blanket spread, ample brownish woolen
    blanket,
Gray and heavy blanket, folding, covering all.

Curious I halt and silent stand,
Then with light fingers I from the face of the nearest the
    first just lift the blanket;
Who are you elderly man so gaunt and grim, with well-
    gray'd hair, and flesh all sunken about the eyes?
Who are you my dear comrade?

Then to the second I step—and who are you my child and
    darling?
Who are you sweet boy with cheeks yet blooming?

Then to the third—a face nor child nor old, very calm,
    as of beautiful yellow-white ivory;
Young man I think I know you—I think this face is the
    face of the Christ himself,
Dead and divine and brother of all, and here again he lies.


## Reconciliation

WORD over all, beautiful as the sky,
Beautiful that war and all its deeds of carnage must in time
    be utterly lost,

That the hands of the sisters Death and Night incessantly
    softly wash again, and ever again, this soil'd world;
For my enemy is dead, a man divine as myself is dead,
I look where he lies white-faced and still in the coffin—
    I draw near,
Bend down and touch lightly with my lips the white face
    in the coffin.


## A Noiseless Patient Spider

A NOISELESS patient spider,
I mark'd where on a little promontory it stood isolated,
Mark'd how to explore the vacant vast surrounding,
It launched forth filament, filament, filament, out of itself,
Ever unreeling them, ever tirelessly speeding them.

And you O my soul where you stand,
Surrounded, detached, in measureless oceans of space,
Ceaselessly musing, venturing, throwing, seeking the spheres
    to connect them,
Till the bridge you will need be form'd, till the ductile
    anchor hold,
Till the gossamer thread you fling catch somewhere, O my
    soul.


## Sparkles from the Wheel

WHERE the city's ceaseless crowd moves on the livelong day,
Withdrawn I join a group of children watching, I pause
    aside with them.

By the curb toward the edge of the flagging,
A knife-grinder works at his wheel sharpening a great knife,
Bending over he carefully holds it to the stone, by foot and
    knee,
With measur'd tread he turns rapidly, as he presses with
    light but firm hand,
Forth issue then in copious golden jets,
Sparkles from the wheel.

The scene and all its belongings, how they seize and affect
    me,
The sad sharp-chinn'd old man with worn clothes and broad
    shoulder-band of leather,
Myself effusing and fluid, a phantom curiously floating,
    now here absorb'd and arrested,
The group, (an unminded point set in a vast surrounding,)
The attentive, quiet children, the loud, proud, restive base
    of the streets,
The low hoarse purr of the whirling stone, the light-press'd
    blade,
Diffusing, dropping, sideways-darting, in tiny showers of
    gold,
Sparkles from the wheel.

## The Dismantled Ship

IN some unused lagoon, some nameless bay,
On sluggish, lonesome waters, anchor'd near the shore,
An old, dismasted, gray and batter'd ship, disabled, done,
After free voyages to all the seas of earth, haul'd up at last
    and hawser'd tight,
Lies rusting, mouldering.

# EMILY DICKINSON

## 1830–1886

Daughter of a stiff, conservative small-town New England lawyer and sometime Congressman, Emily Dickinson lived all her life in her father's house in Amherst, Massachusetts, in later years never venturing outside the door. She never married and lived a life, as she once wrote, "too simple and stern to embarrass any." She was known to write occasional verses, a few of which had been published, but even her sister and lifelong companion was astonished to discover after her death the neat manuscripts of some 1775 poems or fragments of poems. These manuscripts, after long adventures that cannot be detailed here, have finally been published fully and correctly, as have her surviving letters. These, with the researches of biographers, now make it possible to see with some clearness the extraordinary inner life of this solitary recluse.

A key word in this lonely life was love. Though she gave her heart more than once and entirely, she never had a "love affair" as the world understands such things. Something in her made certain that she would love only where fulfillment was impossible. One need not indulge in Freudian speculations to notice that she loved only men whom she could imagine in the role of a father. This clearly was true of the great love of her life, the dedicated, married, middle-aged Philadelphia preacher, Charles Wadsworth, who plays a lover's role in some of her poems which this exemplary man most certainly did not play in life. She could not have seen him more than three or four times in her lifetime. Yet the passion she conceived for him not merely underlies most of her poems of love, but the terror she felt when she first heard, in 1861, that he would soon "leave the land" and go to California was one main cause for the astounding flood of poems that burst from her in the next few years. As she once said, the "death-blow" to her life was a "life-blow" to her mind.

"Be one of those," wrote Henry James, "on whom nothing is lost." No one has ever followed this advice more fully than Emily Dickinson. The intensity of feeling and thought radiating from her concentrated poems would leave us "bare and charred" if we were not, in our preoccupation, such poor conductors. For her the smallest event was momentous. If her subjects are of the village her language draws on all the world: the pomp of royalty, the pageantry of history, the romance of geography all contribute to magnify her encounter with butterfly or hummingbird, just as metaphors from her woman's household life give actuality to large topics. In the manner of the Calvinism in which she was reared but which she never accepted, she felt each hour to be the brink of eternity. Appropriately, she did not try to write hypnotic verse, like Poe or Whitman, but rather a poetry of definition. Many of her poems *are* definitions, succinct summaries of the truths she was wringing from life. All characteristically make sudden witty conjunctions that startle the mind into a full awareness of what she is trying to say. Her style is essentially metaphysical, like Donne's, rather than romantic.

She seems to have been largely unaware of her membership in a special tradition; her literary tastes, by and large, were those of any educated lady of her day—Romantics and Victorians, mostly, with a special interest in Elizabeth Barrett Browning and the Brontë sisters—and her forms were not the elaborate stanzas of the seventeenth century but usually the simplest she knew, the 4–3 and 4–4 ballad forms of the hymns of her childhood, though she had trouble fitting her thought to their small measure and developed an original habit of half-rhyming in order to do so. Her diction was also original, at times almost a special language of her own, whose unexpected juxtapositions, though sometimes merely coy or eccentric, often succeed in saying in a few words what ordinary speech would take lines to explain. Here again her difference seems to have been unintended and unguided: "All men say 'What?' to me," she complained plaintively to a correspondent. For all her shyness and modesty, however, she clearly had little doubt that her difference from ordinary men was a superiority. She refused to publish partly because she correctly assumed that the public of her day would not understand her. She will always have "fit audience though few," for she is the most spiritually demanding, as well as one of the most rewarding, of American authors.

BIBLIOGRAPHY: Thomas H. Johnson, *The Poems of Emily Dickinson* (Cambridge, Mass., 1955) and *The Letters of Emily Dickinson* (Cambridge, Mass., 1958) are the only editions in which she should be read. All others are superseded. For biography, George F. Whicher, *This Was a Poet* (New York, 1938) is still good, as is T. H. Johnson, *Emily Dickinson* (Cambridge, Mass., 1955). The best account of the publication of the poems is Millicent Bingham, *Ancestors' Brocades* (New York, 1945). A recent critical treatment is Charles R. Anderson, *Emily Dickinson's Poetry* (New York, 1960); Allen Tate's "Emily Dickinson" in *The Man of Letters in the Modern World* (Meridian Books, New York, 1955) is well known. The present text follows Johnson's exactly, with all its manuscript peculiarities, since that is the text the poet left us.

## 'Success is counted sweetest'

SUCCESS is counted sweetest
By those who ne'er succeed.
To comprehend a nectar
Requires sorest need.

Not one of all the purple Host
Who took the Flag today
Can tell the definition
So clear of Victory

As he defeated – dying –
On whose forbidden ear
The distant strains of triumph
Burst agonized and clear!

## 'I taste a liquor never brewed'

I TASTE a liquor never brewed –
From Tankards scooped in Pearl –
Not all the Vats upon the Rhine
Yield such an Alcohol!

Inebriate of Air – am I –
And Debauchee of Dew –
Reeling – thro endless summer days –
From inns of Molten Blue –

When "Landlords" turn the drunken Bee
Out of the Foxglove's door –
When Butterflies – renounce their "drams" –
I shall but drink the more!

Till Seraphs swing their snowy Hats –
And Saints – to windows run –
To see the little Tippler
Leaning against the – Sun –


## 'Safe in their Alabaster Chambers'

SAFE in their Alabaster Chambers –
Untouched by Morning
And untouched by Noon –
Sleep the meek members of the Resurrection –
Rafter of satin,
And Roof of stone.

Light laughs the breeze
In her Castle above them –
Babbles the Bee in a stolid Ear,
Pipe the Sweet Birds in ignorant cadence –
Ah, what sagacity perished here!


## 'There's a certain Slant of light'

THERE'S a certain Slant of light,
Winter Afternoons –
That oppresses, like the Heft
Of Cathedral Tunes –

Heavenly Hurt, it gives us –
We can find no scar,
But internal difference,
Where the Meanings, are –

None may teach it – Any –
'Tis the Seal Despair –
An imperial affliction
Sent us of the Air –

When it comes, the Landscape listens –
Shadows – hold their breath –
When it goes, 'tis like the Distance
On the look of Death –


## 'The Soul selects her own Society'

THE Soul selects her own Society –
Then – shuts the Door –
To her divine Majority –
Present no more –

Unmoved – she notes the Chariots – pausing –
At her low Gate –
Unmoved – an Emperor be kneeling
Upon her Mat –

I've known her – from an ample nation –
Choose One –
Then – close the Valves of her attention –
Like Stone –


## 'A Bird came down the Walk'

A BIRD came down the Walk –
He did not know I saw –
He bit an Angleworm in halves
And ate the fellow, raw,

And then he drank a Dew
From a convenient Grass –
And then hopped sidewise to the Wall
To let a Beetle pass –

He glanced with rapid eyes
That hurried all around –
They looked like frightened Beads, I thought –
He stirred his Velvet Head

Like one in danger, Cautious,
I offered him a Crumb
And he unrolled his feathers
And rowed him softer home –

Than Oars divide the Ocean,
Too silver for a seam –
Or Butterflies, off Banks of Noon
Leap, plashless as they swim.

## 'The Heart asks Pleasure – first'

THE Heart asks Pleasure – first –
And then – Excuse from Pain –
And then – those little Anodynes
That deaden suffering –

And then – to go to sleep –
And then – if it should be
The will of it's Inquisitor
The privilege to die –

## 'Of all the Souls that stand create'

OF all the Souls that stand create –
I have elected – One –
When Sense from Spirit – files away –
And Subterfuge – is done –
When that which is – and that which was –
Apart – intrinsic – stand –
And this brief Tragedy of Flesh –
Is shifted – like a Sand –
When Figures show their royal Front –
And Mists – are carved away,
Behold the Atom – I preferred –
To all the lists of Clay!

## 'Their Hight in Heaven comforts not'

THEIR Hight in Heaven comforts not –
Their Glory – nought to me –
'Twas best imperfect – as it was –
I'm finite – I cant see –

The House of Supposition –
The Glimmering Frontier that
skirts the Acres of Perhaps –
To Me – shows insecure –

The Wealth I had – contented me –
If 'twas a meaner size –
Then I had counted it until
It pleased my narrow Eyes –

Better than larger values –
That show however true –
This timid life of Evidence
Keeps pleading – "I dont know."

## 'Because I could not stop for Death'

BECAUSE I could not stop for Death –
He kindly stopped for me –
The Carriage held but just Ourselves –
And Immortality.

We slowly drove – He knew no haste
And I had put away
My labor and my leisure too,
For His Civility –

We passed the School, where Children strove
At Recess – in the Ring –
We passed the Fields of Gazing Grain –
We passed the Setting Sun –

Or rather – He passed Us –
The Dews drew quivering and chill –
For only Gossamer, my Gown –
My Tippet – only Tulle –

We paused before a House that seemed
A Swelling of the Ground –
The Roof was scarcely visible –
The Cornice – in the Ground –

Since then – 'tis Centuries – and yet
Feels shorter than the Day
I first surmised the Horses Heads
Were toward Eternity –

## 'This quiet Dust was Gentlemen and Ladies'

THIS quiet Dust was Gentlemen and Ladies
And Lads and Girls –
Was laughter and ability and Sighing
And Frocks and Curls.

This Passive Place a Summer's nimble mansion
Where Bloom and Bees
Exist an Oriental Circuit
Then cease, like these –

## 'A narrow Fellow in the Grass'

A NARROW Fellow in the Grass
Occasionally rides –
You may have met Him – did you not
His notice sudden is –

The Grass divides as with a Comb –
A spotted shaft is seen –
And then it closes at your feet
And opens further on –

He likes a Boggy Acre
A Floor too cool for Corn –
Yet when a Boy, and Barefoot –

I more than once at Noon
Have passed, I thought, a Whip lash
Unbraiding in the Sun
When stooping to secure it
It wrinkled, and was gone –

Several of Nature's People
I know, and they know me –
I feel for them a transport
Of cordiality –

But never met this Fellow
Attended, or alone
Without a tighter breathing
And Zero at the Bone –

## 'Tell all the Truth but tell it slant'

TELL all the Truth but tell it slant –
Success in Circuit lies
Too bright for our infirm Delight
The Truth's superb surprise
As Lightning to the Children eased
With explanation kind
The Truth must dazzle gradually
Or every man be blind –

## 'A Route of Evanescence'

A ROUTE of Evanescence
With a revolving Wheel –
A Resonance of Emerald –

A Rush of Cochineal –
And every Blossom on the Bush
Adjusts it's tumbled Head –
The mail from Tunis, probably,
An easy Morning's Ride –


### 'My life closed twice before its close'

MY life closed twice before its close;
It yet remains to see
If Immortality unveil
A third event to me,

So huge, so hopeless to conceive
As these that twice befel.
Parting is all we know of heaven,
And all we need of hell.


### 'Essential Oils – are wrung'

Essential Oils – are wrung –
The Attar from the Rose
Be not expressed by suns – alone –
It is the gift of Screws –

The General Rose – decay –
But this – in Lady's Drawer
Make Summer – When the Lady lie
In Ceaseless Rosemary –

# EDWIN ARLINGTON ROBINSON

## 1869–1935

In Dickinson, Robinson, and Frost we have a series of instinctively conservative New Englanders who became innovators almost in spite of themselves, following the path Frost called "the old way to be new." Robinson's verse shows the influence of the reigning poets of his time, chiefly Browning and Hardy, and more incongruously the dainty villanelles and rondeaus of Austin Dobson and Edmund Gosse. In his hands, however, the old forms all learned a new voice. Like Milton, Wordsworth, or T. S. Eliot, he was an example of the "egotistical sublime" who imposed his spirit on everything he wrote. At the same time, he was a dramatic poet who preferred to speak through masks and created a whole gallery of characters, all in their variety still resembling their author. A taste for Robinson must rest on an appreciation of his "angle of vision": tragic, philosophic, ironic, austere yet argumentative, a special blend of dark doubt and last-ditch faith.

Reared in Gardiner, Maine—the prototype of his "Tilbury Town"—and educated at *fin de siècle* Harvard, he reflected and often argued at length in his poems a world view that can be described as the last stand of New England Idealism against the encroachments of Darwinian pessimism. Like such predecessors as Emerson and Thoreau—represented in this volume by the New Yorker, Whitman—he believed in an inner Light or Word which certified directly to the heart of the individual a divine Presence within and beyond the world of ordinary experience. At the same time, when he looked around him he did not see evidences of this God in everything, as did Whitman, but rather "The black and awful chaos of the night"; or as he put it succinctly in a letter, "a hell of a place." His life did not encourage him to see it as much else, being a long struggle against poverty, drink, and the indifference of his townsmen and countrymen to his poetic calling. Even the odd circumstance of being publicly praised by the President of the United States, Theodore Roosevelt, did not help his critical reputation, which was not firmly established until the success of his long Arthurian poem, *Tristram,* in 1928. In view of his bleak history, the honesty with which he continued to confront the facts and the courage with which he continued to insist that they were no ground for despair are both admirable.

In general, those poems in which he argues these issues directly are among his least interesting. Though concerned with ultimate questions, he disliked to be called a "philosophic" poet and did not in fact show any special profundity or consistency. He was a poet and a dramatist, not a thinker, and his work will live in those poems in which he presents lives, not Life. Like Faulkner, he created an imaginary region in the image of his early home and peopled it with what Hardy would call "destinies." Like their author, they tend to be "men against the sky"—single figures confronting Fate. There is Luke Havergal, facing the loss of his love; Richard Cory, realizing the emptiness of "success"; Annandale in his last agonizing illness; Flammonde, the Prince of Castaways; or Mr. Flood, whose only surviving boon companion is himself. Life promises nothing to any of these any more, yet each in his own way has the heroic sense that marks all the characters of whom Robinson approves, a tragic dignity, like the dark hills of his typical landscape, that is as often expressed in sympathetic humor as in high seriousness. Those of his characters who are too mean-spirited to share this view of life are treated ironically, like Miniver Cheevy, the drunken dreamer, or with savage satire, like the unnamed hypocrite of "Karma." Longer monologues, which cannot be represented here, dramatize the dedication of men "whom a god has chosen"—Rembrandt, Shakespeare, St. Paul, John Brown; and Robinson's epic sense of life flowered naturally in later years in highly original treatments, prolix but impressive, of legends such as the Arthurian stories and of original allegories of his own. He combatted the naturalistic disillusion of his day, not by arguing that human life is happy, since it plainly is not, but by dramatizing the significance of the individual destiny. "We begin to live," Yeats has written, "when we have conceived life as tragedy." In the same spirit Robinson's somber poems, as he hoped, do more than the "positive thinking" of those who rejected him, to give "an impression that life is very much worth while."

BIBLIOGRAPHY: The standard edition is *Collected Poems* (New York, 1939); the standard biography that of Herman Hagedorn (New York, 1938). Robinson's letters are surprisingly warm and revealing; see *Selected Letters of Edward Arlington Robinson* (New York, 1940). Yvor Winters' little book (Norfolk, Conn., 1946) shows his usual intelligence and assurance. A useful recent study is by Ellsworth Barnard (New York, 1952).

## Walt Whitman

THE master-songs are ended, and the man
That sang them is a name. And so is God
A name; and so is love, and life, and death,
And everything. But we, who are too blind
To read what we have written, or what faith
Has written for us, do not understand:
We only blink, and wonder.

Last night it was the song that was the man,
But now it is the man that is the song.
We do not hear him very much to-day:
His piercing and eternal cadence rings
Too pure for us—too powerfully pure,
Too lovingly triumphant, and too large;
But there are some that hear him, and they know
That he shall sing to-morrow for all men,
And that all time shall listen.

The master-songs are ended? Rather say
No songs are ended that are ever sung,
And that no names are dead names. When we write
Men's letters on proud marble or on sand,
We write them there forever.

## Luke Havergal

Go to the western gate, Luke Havergal,
There where the vines cling crimson on the wall,
And in the twilight wait for what will come.
The leaves will whisper there of her, and some,
Like flying words, will strike you as they fall;
But go, and if you listen she will call.

Go to the western gate, Luke Havergal—
Luke Havergal.

No, there is not a dawn in eastern skies
To rift the fiery night that's in your eyes;
But there, where western glooms are gathering,
The dark will end the dark, if anything:
God slays Himself with every leaf that flies,
And hell is more than half of paradise.
No, there is not a dawn in eastern skies—
In eastern skies.

Out of a grave I come to tell you this,
Out of a grave I come to quench the kiss
That flames upon your forehead with a glow
That blinds you to the way that you must go.
Yes, there is yet one way to where she is,
Bitter, but one that faith may never miss.
Out of a grave I come to tell you this—
To tell you this.

There is the western gate, Luke Havergal,
There are the crimson leaves upon the wall.
Go, for the winds are tearing them away,—
Nor think to riddle the dead words they say,
Nor any more to feel them as they fall;
But go, and if you trust her she will call.
There is the western gate, Luke Havergal—
Luke Havergal.


## The House on the Hill

THEY are all gone away,
    The House is shut and still,
There is nothing more to say.

Through broken walls and gray
    The winds blow bleak and shrill:
They are all gone away.

Nor is there one to-day
    To speak them good or ill:
There is nothing more to say.

Why is it then we stray
    Around the sunken sill?
They are all gone away,

And our poor fancy-play
    For them is wasted skill:
There is nothing more to say.

There is ruin and decay
    In the House on the Hill:
They are all gone away,
There is nothing more to say.


## *Richard Cory*

WHENEVER Richard Cory went down town,
We people on the pavement looked at him:
He was a gentleman from sole to crown,
Clean favored, and imperially slim.

And he was always quietly arrayed,
And he was always human when he talked;
But still he fluttered pulses when he said,
'Good-morning,' and he glittered when he walked.

And he was rich—yes, richer than a king—
And admirably schooled in every grace:
In fine, we thought that he was everything
To make us wish that we were in his place.

So on we worked, and waited for the light,
And went without the meat, and cursed the bread;
And Richard Cory, one calm summer night,
Went home and put a bullet through his head.

## How Annandale Went Out

"THEY called it Annandale—and I was there
to flourish, to find words, and to attend:
Liar, physician, hypocrite, and friend,
I watched him; and the sight was not so fair
As one or two that I have seen elsewhere:
An apparatus not for me to mend—
A wreck, with hell between him and the end,
Remained of Annandale; and I was there.

"I knew the ruin as I knew the man;
So put the two together, if you can,
Remembering the worst you know of me.
Now view yourself as I was, on the spot—
With a slight kind of engine. Do you see?
Like this . . . You wouldn't hang me? I thought not."

## Miniver Cheevy

MINIVER CHEEVY, child of scorn,
    Grew lean while he assailed the seasons;
He wept that he was ever born,
    And he had reasons.

Miniver loved the days of old
     When swords were bright and steeds were prancing;
The vision of a warrior bold
     Would set him dancing.

Miniver sighed for what was not,
     And dreamed, and rested from his labors;
He dreamed of Thebes and Camelot,
     And Priam's neighbors.

Miniver mourned the ripe renown
     That made so many a name so fragrant;
He mourned Romance, now on the town,
     And Art, a vagrant.

Miniver loved the Medici,
     Albeit he had never seen one;
He would have sinned incessantly
     Could he have been one.

Miniver cursed the commonplace
     And eyed a khaki suit with loathing;
He missed the mediæval grace
     Of iron clothing.

Miniver scorned the gold he sought,
     But sore annoyed was he without it;
Miniver thought, and thought, and thought,
     And thought about it.

Miniver Cheevy, born too late,
     Scratched his head and kept on thinking;
Miniver coughed, and called it fate,
     And kept on drinking.

## *Flammonde*

THE man Flammonde, from God knows where,
With firm address and foreign air,
With news of nations in his talk
And something royal in his walk,
With glint of iron in his eyes,
But never doubt, nor yet surprise,
Appeared, and stayed, and held his head
As one by kings accredited.

Erect, with his alert repose
About him, and about his clothes,
He pictured all tradition hears
Of what we owe to fifty years.
His cleansing heritage of taste
Paraded neither want nor waste;
And what he needed for his fee
To live, he borrowed graciously.

He never told us what he was,
Or what mischance, or other cause,
Had banished him from better days
To play the Prince of Castaways.
Meanwhile he played surpassing well
A part, for most, unplayable;
In fine, one pauses, half afraid
To say for certain that he played.

For that, one may as well forego
Conviction as to yes or no;
Nor can I say just how intense
Would then have been the difference
To several, who, having striven

In vain to get what he was given,
Would see the stranger taken on
By friends not easy to be won.

Moreover, many a malcontent
He soothed and found munificent;
His courtesy beguiled and foiled
Suspicion that his years were soiled;
His mien distinguished any crowd,
His credit strengthened when he bowed;
And women, young and old, were fond
Of looking at the man Flammonde.

There was a woman in our town
On whom the fashion was to frown;
But while our talk renewed the tinge
Of a long-faded scarlet fringe,
The man Flammonde saw none of that,
And what he saw we wondered at—
That none of us, in her distress,
Could hide or find our littleness.

There was a boy that all agreed
Had shut within him the rare seed
Of learning. We could understand,
But none of us could lift a hand.
The man Flammonde appraised the youth,
And told a few of us the truth;
And thereby, for a little gold,
A flowered future was unrolled.

There were two citizens who fought
For years and years, and over nought;
They made life awkward for their friends,

And shortened their own dividends.
The man Flammonde said what was wrong
Should be made right; nor was it long
Before they were again in line,
And had each other in to dine.


And these I mention are but four
Of many out of many more.
So much for them. But what of him—
So firm in every look and limb?
What small satanic sort of kink
Was in his brain? What broken link
Withheld him from the destinies
That came so near to being his?


What was he, when we came to sift
His meaning, and to note the drift
Of incommunicable ways
That make us ponder while we praise?
Why was it that his charm revealed
Somehow the surface of a shield?
What was it that we never caught?
What was he, and what was he not?


How much it was of him we met
We cannot ever know; nor yet
Shall all he gave us quite atone
For what was his, and his alone;
Nor need we now, since he knew best,
Nourish an ethical unrest:
Rarely at once will nature give
The power to be Flammonde and live.

We cannot know how much we learn
From those who never will return,
Until a flash of unforeseen
Remembrance falls on what has been.
We've each a darkening hill to climb;
And this is why, from time to time
In Tilbury Town, we look beyond
Horizons for the man Flammonde.

## The Dark Hills

DARK hills at evening in the west,
Where sunset hovers like a sound
Of golden horns that sang to rest
Old bones of warriors under ground,
Far now from all the bannered ways
Where flash the legions of the sun,
You fade—as if the last of days
Were fading, and all wars were done.

## Mr. Flood's Party

OLD Eben Flood, climbing alone one night
Over the hill between the town below
And the forsaken upland hermitage
That held as much as he should ever know
On earth again of home, paused warily.
The road was his with not a native near;
And Eben, having leisure, said aloud,
For no man else in Tilbury Town to hear:

'Well, Mr. Flood, we have the harvest moon
Again, and we may not have many more;
The bird is on the wing, the poet says,
And you and I have said it here before.
Drink to the bird.' He raised up to the light
The jug that he had gone so far to fill,
And answered huskily: 'Well, Mr. Flood,
Since you propose it, I believe I will.'

Alone, as if enduring to the end
A valiant armor of scarred hopes outworn,
He stood there in the middle of the road
Like Roland's ghost winding a silent horn.
Below him, in the town among the trees,
Where friends of other days had honored him,
A phantom salutation of the dead
Rang thinly till old Eben's eyes were dim.

Then, as a mother lays her sleeping child
Down tenderly, fearing it may awake,
He set the jug down slowly at his feet
With trembling care, knowing that most things break;
And only when assured that on firm earth
It stood, as the uncertain lives of men
Assuredly did not, he paced away,
And with his hand extended paused again:

'Well, Mr. Flood, we have not met like this
In a long time; and many a change has come
To both of us, I fear, since last it was
We had a drop together. Welcome home!'
Convivially  returning with himself,
Again he raised the jug up to the light;
And with an acquiescent quaver said:
'Well, Mr. Flood, if you insist, I might.

'Only a very little, Mr. Flood—
'For auld lang syne. No more, sir; that will do.'
So, for the time, apparently it did,
And Eben evidently thought so too;
For soon amid the silver loneliness
Of night he lifted up his voice and sang,
Secure, with only two moons listening,
Until the whole harmonious landscape rang—

'For auld lang syne.' The weary throat gave out,
The last word wavered, and the song was done.
He raised again the jug regretfully
And shook his head, and was again alone.
There was not much that was ahead of him,
And there was nothing in the town below—
Where strangers would have shut the many doors
That many friends had opened long ago.

## Many Are Called

THE Lord Apollo, who has never died,
Still holds alone his immemorial reign,
Supreme in an impregnable domain
That with his magic he has fortified;
And though melodious multitudes have tried
In ecstasy, in anguish, and in vain,
With invocation sacred and profane
To lure him, even the loudest are outside.

Only at unconjectured intervals,
By will of him on whom no man may gaze,
By word of him whose law no man has read,
A questing light may rift the sullen walls,
To cling where mostly its infrequent rays
Fall golden on the patience of the dead.

## The Sheaves

WHERE long the shadows of the wind had rolled,
Green wheat was yielding to the change assigned,
And as by some vast magic undivined
The world was turning slowly into gold.
Like nothing that was ever bought or sold
It waited there, the body and the mind;
And with a mighty meaning of a kind
That tells the more the more it is not told.

So in a land where all days are not fair,
Fair days went on till on another day
A thousand golden sheaves were lying there,
Shining and still, but not for long to stay—
As if a thousand girls with golden hair
Might rise from where they slept and go away.

## Karma

CHRISTMAS was in the air and all was well
With him, but for a few confusing flaws
In divers of God's images. Because
A friend of his would neither buy nor sell,
Was he to answer for the axe that fell?
He pondered; and the reason for it was,
Partly, a slowly freezing Santa Claus
Upon the corner, with his beard and bell.

Acknowledging an improvident surprise,
He magnified a fancy that he wished
The friend whom he had wrecked were here again.
Not sure of that, he found a compromise;
And from the fulness of his heart he fished
A dime for Jesus who had died for men.

# ROBERT FROST

Born 1875

The most important American poet since Whitman is the New Englander, Robert Frost. Many critics have had difficulty grasping this fact, since Frost is deceptively simple and peculiarly regional. Frost also has his legend, one not far from the truth—the farmer-poet who through long years of hardship held fast to his poetic vocation, until finally, having sold his farm and traveled to England on the proceeds, with no resources for the future and a family to support, he won recognition at the age of nearly forty with his first two volumes of verse and returned to America to find himself famous. His subjects are often "North of Boston," though less often in recent years than they used to be, and the language of his verse reflects the idiom and intonation of that region, as was inevitable in view of his determination to practice what Wordsworth preached and build his verse entirely on "the real language of men." Both in themes and technique his verse has been very little affected by the shaping influences on modernist verse—Imagism, Yeats, Eliot, Auden. As any reader of his first book, *A Boy's Will,* can plainly see, his mature style grew gradually from the tone and diction of later nineteenth-century romantic verse. Though his development has paralleled the revolution of modern verse he has not participated in it and belongs essentially to an older tradition. His work is an end or completion rather than a beginning, as his imitators continue to make evident.

Frost's work falls broadly into three categories: dramatic

poems, lyrics, and an intermediate genre of the sort which Coleridge called the "conversation poem." The dramatic poems, of which the early "Home Burial" is one of the best, are more realistic and objective and more socially minded than Robinson's. Where Robinson deals with Fate Frost deals with character. His little dramas either present one of those key moments in a relationship that reveal its essential character or else sketch a personality, usually through the eyes of a sympathetic onlooker. They are conspicuously not "local color" pieces, the treatment of regional "types" by an observer from a more sophisticated world, but assume the full human equality of author, subject and reader. In spite of an apparent detachment and reserve, they radiate a special spirit, both warm and "tough," neither sentimental nor disillusioned, which like their author can have a peculiar magnetism.

The conversation pieces, like "Birches," are familiar essays in verse and succeed like their prose counterparts by the relationship they create between author and reader. To say this is not to suggest, however, that either these essays or the dramatic pieces might as well be written in prose. Frost shares the general aim of modern poets, in the words of Yeats, "to strip away everything that was artificial, to get a style like speech, as simple as the simplest prose, like a cry of the heart." In his case, however, as in that of Yeats, he has thought of the established forms of English verse, not as artificial, but as the tested means by which speech becomes poetry. Poetry is made, he feels, from "the dramatic tones of meaning struck across the rigidity of a limited meter." From the natural speech cadences and vocabulary of his poems the slight heightening at moments, as the poetry rises on the rhythm of the formal movement to meet a climax in the emotion, is extraordinarily affecting to those who have adjusted their ear to the apparent bareness of the whole.

In truth, Frost is perhaps the most classical of American authors. He had a sound classical education and knows his Latin poets well. Some of his poems slyly fall into classical cadences to be appreciated by properly educated readers. Of more importance is the instinctive decorum and restraint that he brings to all his best work. These qualities come out particularly in his lyrics. These are generally in a minor key and treat by means of a few simple natural symbols—rain, wind, snow, leaves, trees, darkness, etc.—an elegiac theme, but they are saved from softness by their strong sense of form and by a resilient self-control that confronts the human condition with human courage.

The range of Frost's poems is represented in this selection on the one hand by the bleak scene in "Desert Places," on the other by the warmth of such a poem as "Birches." Man is encamped in the universe like a traveler on a vast plain. His campfire holds the dark at bay, but it surrounds him, stretching as far as thought can reach, and waits. In a poem like "Desert Places" the outer dark invades his spirit and nearly puts out his center of light altogether, though at the end of the poem he summons some resistance. The threat of the same invasion lurks in poem after poem, even the apparently untroubled "Stopping by Woods," where the lure of "the terrible that attracts and repels," as Ibsen put it, is felt in its most disarming form. Men seek of course to look "out far and in deep," but their stare sees emptiness, or their own image, or ambiguous hints that cannot be deciphered. Autumn is a favorite season in these poems, the fall of the leaves, the descent of rain and darkness, the coming of the snow. But if one pole in Frost's work is Not-Home, the outer dark, the other is Home, the light and warmth that man can make for himself. Home is the house, the family, friends; it is the stability of nature; it is the aftershine of Christianity; it is the memory of youth, before the dark is first seen; it is the power of creating form from chaos; it is love; above all it is the spring of courage inside a man that gives him the strength to love life in spite of his knowledge of dark and make a home for himself in a world unaware of him. Frost is the finest representative in poetry of that great generation of Americans, before our modern failure of nerve, who faced squarely the plain fact that man is alone in a mysterious universe that contains nothing of value except what he can make of it, and could say, as Frost does, "What pleasanter than that this should be so?"

BIBLIOGRAPHY: The *Complete Poems* have been put out by Henry Holt (New York, 1949); his extraordinary prose is uncollected. Frost's powerful personality has so overwhelmed admirers and detractors alike that a proper criticism of his poetry has hardly begun. The first biography of any importance is Elizabeth Shepley Sergeant, *Robert Frost; The Trial by Existence* (New York, 1960). His official biographer-to-be, Lawrance Thompson, has written a book, *Fire and Ice* (New York, 1942) and a pamphlet, *Robert Frost* (University of Minnesota, 1959). Two very recent studies are John F. Lynen, *The Pastoral Art of Robert Frost* (Yale, 1960) and George W. Nitchie, *Human Values in the Poetry of Robert Frost* (Duke University, 1960). The best appreciative articles in book form, in spite of an effervescence that grows tiresome, are those by Randall Jarrell in his *Poetry and the Age* (New York, 1953).

## *Home Burial*

HE saw her from the bottom of the stairs
Before she saw him. She was starting down,
Looking back over her shoulder at some fear.
She took a doubtful step and then undid it
To raise herself and look again. He spoke
Advancing toward her: "What is it you see
From up there always—for I want to know."
She turned and sank upon her skirts at that,
And her face turned from terrified to dull.
He said to gain time: "What is it you see,"
Mounting until she cowered under him.
"I will find out now—you must tell me, dear."
She, in her place, refused him any help
With the least stiffening of her neck and silence.
She let him look, sure that he wouldn't see,
Blind creature; and a while he didn't see.
But at last he murmured, "Oh," and again, "Oh."

"What is it—what?" she said.

                              "Just that I see."

"You don't," she challenged. "Tell me what it is."

"The wonder is I didn't see at once.
I never noticed it from here before.
I must be wonted to it—that's the reason.
The little graveyard where my people are!
So small the window frames the whole of it.
Not so much larger than a bedroom, is it?
There are three stones of slate and one of marble,
Broad-shouldered little slabs there in the sunlight
On the sidehill. We haven't to mind *those*.

But I understand: it's not the stones,
But the child's mound——"

   "Don't, don't, don't, don't," she cried.

She withdrew shrinking from beneath his arm
That rested on the banister, and slid downstairs;
And turned on him with such a daunting look,
He said twice over before he knew himself:
"Can't a man speak of his own child he's lost?"

"Not you! Oh, where's my hat? Oh, I don't need it!
I must get out of here. I must get air.
I don't know rightly whether any man can."

"Amy! Don't go to someone else this time.
Listen to me. I won't come down the stairs."
He sat and fixed his chin between his fists.
"There's something I should like to ask you, dear."

"You don't know how to ask it."

   "Help me, then."

Her fingers moved the latch for all reply.

"My words are nearly always an offence.
I don't know how to speak of anything
So as to please you. But I might be taught
I should suppose. I can't say I see how.
A man must partly give up being a man
With women-folk. We could have some arrangement
By which I'd bind myself to keep hands off
Anything special you're a-mind to name.
Though I don't like such things 'twixt those that love.
Two that don't love can't live together without them.

But two that do can't live together with them."
She moved the latch a little. "Don't—don't go.
Don't carry it to someone else this time.
Tell me about it if it's something human.
Let me into your grief. I'm not so much
Unlike other folks as your standing there
Apart would make me out. Give me my chance.
I do think, though, you overdo it a little.
What was it brought you up to think it the thing
To take your mother-loss of a first child
So inconsolably—in the face of love.
You'd think his memory might be satisfied—"

"There you go sneering now!"

"I'm not, I'm not!
You make me angry. I'll come down to you.
God, what a woman! And it's come to this,
A man can't speak of his own child that's dead."

"You can't because you don't know how.
If you had any feelings, you that dug
With your own hand—how could you?—his little grave;
I saw you from that very window there,
Making the gravel leap and leap in air,
Leap up, like that, like that, and land so lightly
And roll back down the mound beside the hole.
I thought, Who is that man? I don't know you.
And I crept down the stairs and up the stairs
To look again, and still your spade kept lifting.
Then you came in. I heard your rumbling voice
Out in the kitchen, and I don't know why,
But I went near to see with my own eyes.

You could sit there with the stains on your shoes
Of the fresh earth from your own baby's grave
And talk about your everyday concerns.
You had stood the spade up against the wall
Outside there in the entry, for I saw it."

"I shall laugh the worst laugh I ever laughed.
I'm cursed. God, if I don't believe I'm cursed."

"I can repeat the very words you were saying.
'Three foggy mornings and one rainy day
Will rot the best birch fence a man can build.'
Think of it, talk like that at such a time!
What had how long it takes a birch to rot
To do with what was in the darkened parlour.
You *couldn't* care! The nearest friends can go
With anyone to death, comes so far short
They might as well not try to go at all.
No, from the time when one is sick to death,
One is alone, and he dies more alone.
Friends make pretence of following to the grave,
But before one is in it, their minds are turned
And making the best of their way back to life
And living people, and things they understand.
But the world's evil. I won't have grief so
If I can change it. Oh, I won't, I won't!"

"There, you have said it all and you feel better.
You won't go now. You're crying. Close the door.
The heart's gone out of it: why keep it up.
Amy! There's someone coming down the road!"

"*You*—oh, you think the talk is all. I must go—
Somewhere out of this house. How can I make you—"

"If—you—do!" She was opening the door wider.
"Where do you mean to go? First tell me that.
I'll follow and bring you back by force. I *will!*—"


## The Road Not Taken

Two roads diverged in a yellow wood,
And sorry I could not travel both
And be one traveler, long I stood
And looked down one as far as I could
To where it bent in the undergrowth;


Then took the other, as just as fair,
And having perhaps the better claim,
Because it was grassy and wanted wear;
Though as for that the passing there
Had worn them really about the same,


And both that morning equally lay
In leaves no step had trodden black.
Oh, I kept the first for another day!
Yet knowing how way leads on to way,
I doubted if I should ever come back.


I shall be telling this with a sigh
Somewhere ages and ages hence:
Two roads diverged in a wood, and I—
I took the one less traveled by,
And that has made all the difference.

## Birches

WHEN I see birches bend to left and right
Across the lines of straighter darker trees,
I like to think some boy's been swinging them.
But swinging doesn't bend them down to stay.
Ice-storms do that. Often you must have seen them
Loaded with ice a sunny winter morning
After a rain. They click upon themselves
As the breeze rises, and turn many-colored
As the stir cracks and crazes their enamel.
Soon the sun's warmth makes them shed crystal shells
Shattering and avalanching on the snow-crust—
Such heaps of broken glass to sweep away
You'd think the inner dome of heaven had fallen.
They are dragged to the withered bracken by the load,
And they seem not to break; though once they are bowed
So low for long, they never right themselves:
You may see their trunks arching in the woods
Years afterwards, trailing their leaves on the ground
Like girls on hands and knees that throw their hair
Before them over their heads to dry in the sun.
But I was going to say when Truth broke in
With all her matter-of-fact about the ice-storm
I should prefer to have some boy bend them
As he went out and in to fetch the cows—
Some boy too far from town to learn baseball,
Whose only play was what he found himself,
Summer or winter, and could play alone.
One by one he subdued his father's trees
By riding them down over and over again
Until he took the stiffness out of them,
And not one but hung limp, not one was left
For him to conquer. He learned all there was

To learn about not launching out too soon
And so not carrying the tree away
Clear to the ground. He always kept his poise
To the top branches, climbing carefully
With the same pains you use to fill a cup
Up to the brim, and even above the brim.
Then he flung outward, feet first, with a swish,
Kicking his way down through the air to the ground.
So was I once myself a swinger of birches.
And so I dream of going back to be.
It's when I'm weary of considerations,
And life is too much like a pathless wood
Where your face burns and tickles with the cobwebs
Broken across it, and one eye is weeping
From a twig's having lashed across it open.
I'd like to get away from earth awhile
And then come back to it and begin over.
May no fate willfully misunderstand me
And half grant what I wish and snatch me away
Not to return. Earth's the right place for love:
I don't know where it's likely to go better.
I'd like to go by climbing a birch tree,
And climb black branches up a snow-white trunk
*Toward* heaven, till the tree could bear no more,
But dipped its top and set me down again.
That would be good both going and coming back.
One could do worse than be a swinger of birches.

## Fire and Ice

SOME say the world will end in fire,
Some say in ice.
From what I've tasted of desire
I hold with those who favor fire.

But if it had to perish twice,
I think I know enough of hate
To say that for destruction ice
Is also great
And would suffice.

## Stopping by Woods on a Snowy Evening

WHOSE woods these are I think I know.
His house is in the village though;
He will not see me stopping here
To watch his woods fill up with snow.

My little horse must think it queer
To stop without a farmhouse near
Between the woods and frozen lake
The darkest evening of the year.

He gives his harness bells a shake
To ask if there is some mistake.
The only other sound's the sweep
Of easy wind and downy flake.

The woods are lovely, dark and deep,
But I have promises to keep,
And miles to go before I sleep,
And miles to go before I sleep.

## Desert Places

SNOW falling and night falling fast, oh, fast
In a field I looked into going past,
And the ground almost covered smooth in snow,
But a few weeds and stubble showing last.

The woods around it have it—it is theirs.
All animals are smothered in their lairs.
I am too absent-spirited to count;
The loneliness includes me unawares.

And lonely as it is that loneliness
Will be more lonely ere it will be less—
A blanker whiteness of benighted snow
With no expression, nothing to express.

They cannot scare me with their empty spaces
Between stars—on stars where no human race is.
I have it in me so much nearer home
To scare myself with my own desert places.


## Design

I FOUND a dimpled spider, fat and white,
On a white heal-all, holding up a moth
Like a white piece of rigid satin cloth—
Assorted characters of death and blight
Mixed ready to begin the morning right,
Like the ingredients of a witches' broth—
A snow-drop spider, a flower like froth,
And dead wings carried like a paper kite.

What had that flower to do with being white,
The wayside blue and innocent heal-all?
What brought the kindred spider to that height,
Then steered the white moth thither in the night?
What but design of darkness to appall?—
If design govern in a thing so small.

## Provide Provide

THE witch that came (the withered hag)
To wash the steps with pail and rag,
Was once the beauty Abishag,

The picture pride of Hollywood.
Too many fall from great and good
For you to doubt the likelihood.

Die early and avoid the fate.
Or if predestined to die late,
Make up your mind to die in state.

Make the whole stock exchange your own!
If need be occupy a throne,
Where nobody can call *you* crone.

Some have relied on what they knew;
Others on being simply true.
What worked for them might work for you.

No memory of having starred
Atones for later disregard,
Or keeps the end from being hard.

Better to go down dignified
With boughten friendship at your side
Than none at all. Provide, provide!

## The Gift Outright

THE land was ours before we were the land's.
She was our land more than a hundred years
Before we were her people. She was ours
In Massachusetts, in Virginia,

But we were England's, still colonials,
Possessing what we still were unpossessed by,
Possessed by what we now no more possessed.
Something we were withholding made us weak
Until we found out that it was ourselves
We were withholding from our land of living,
And forthwith found salvation in surrender.
Such as we were we gave ourselves outright
(The deed of gift was many deeds of war)
To the land vaguely realizing westward,
But still unstoried, artless, unenhanced,
Such as she was, such as she would become.

# WALLACE STEVENS

## 1879–1955

Wallace Stevens gives no comfort to those who would weep for the plight of the artist in the modern world, since he reconciled with no apparent conflict or regret a steady, sober career as lawyer in New York and insurance executive in Hartford, Connecticut, with the production of poems which his business associates, if they ever looked at them, surely regarded as not sober at all. Poetry excepted, there was nothing of the Bohemian about Stevens. "It gives a man character as a poet to have a daily contact with a job," he said. "I doubt whether I've lost a thing by leading an exceedingly regular and disciplined life." He and Dylan Thomas, the other great modern poet who died about the same time, shared absolutely nothing at all except a common reputation for being obscure.

Everything Stevens did impresses one as disciplined and deliberate, and the startling eccentricities of his first and best book, *Harmonium,* are no exception. A glance down the table of contents is enough to warn us that we are dealing with a man who intends to be different: "The Comedian as the Letter C"; "The Worms at Heaven's Gate"; "Floral Decorations for Bananas"; "The Emperor of Ice-Cream"; "Thirteen Ways of Looking at a Blackbird"; etc. The content of these poems is often as *outré* as the titles. Yet he can be read, and with a few basic clues and the attention all new art works have a right to ask his poems can reveal themselves as among the most serious and beautiful of modern verse.

The first thing to recognize is that Stevens is a "poet's

poet"; that is, he is as much or more interested in how he writes than in what he has to say. R. P. Blackmur defines him, in the words of Logan Pearsall Smith, as one of "these artists who derive their inspiration more from the formal than the emotional aspects of their art, and who are more interested in the masterly control of their material, than in the expression of their own feelings, or the prophetic aspects of their calling." The open preference in modern abstract painting for a formal rather than a presentational art has had a strong influence on Stevens' verse. Thus the details of Stevens' poetic world, his images and vocabulary, are often precious and exotic, obviously "poetic," as if he wished to insist on the difference between art and life.

Sometimes Stevens' intention, though not vague, is atmospheric and as "irrational" as music. More often, at least in his first book, it is specific enough but conveyed by poetic means, image, symbol and sound, rather than by statement. One main key to his work is to realize that like Yeats, though less systematically, he has built up in his poetry a system of symbols, a kind of private language or poetic shorthand, which we can to a degree translate into lines of meaning. The sun, for example, quite regularly stands for physical reality, the "unthinking source," while the moon presides over the imagination. The colors red and blue have similar opposite connotations. The poet, the man of imagination, is often represented by a performer, a "comedian" or pianist or guitar player. The South is the country of the imagination; Spaniards, the people who are at home in it. The North is "essential prose," yet also the proper home for the Northern poet. These are mere crude notations of the kind of thing to look for; actually, Stevens' symbols are built up within and for each poem, with endless variations, additions, reversals, ironies. The point is that one of his poems helps another, so that the best solution to the problem of reading Stevens is to read him until his special language becomes familiar and transparent. He is one of those poets who are half-destroyed by being anthologized.

A final clue to Stevens is that to a great degree he is a reflexive poet, in the sense that the subject of much of his poetry is poetry. Such a preoccupation is a natural one for the kind of poet we have been describing. In his case it does not lead to a barren formalism, but to an impressive modern restatement of the romantic aesthetic. He begins where the romantics did, with the post-Kantian discovery of the necessary contribution of the imagination to all human perception and knowledge. The world we inhabit is one we "half create"; we make the order we perceive. The poet, then, for Stevens as for Coleridge or Shelley, becomes the archetype of the creative power of thought on which all human understanding depends. Stevens does not, like some romantics, suggest that the human mind can make the world it wills. No poetry is possible without the severe discipline of reality. Stevens' view of man is modern and naturalistic, not the "spilt religion" of the romantics. Like them, however, he asserts the dignity as well as the discipline of the poet. "What makes the poet the potent figure that he is, or was, or ought to be," he writes, "is that he creates the world to which we turn incessantly and without knowing it and that he gives to life the supreme fictions without which we are unable to conceive of it." "I am," his poet asserts,

> I am the necessary angel of the earth,
> Since, in my sight, you see the earth again.

BIBLIOGRAPHY: The *Collected Poems* appeared in 1955; to it should be added *Opus Posthumous*, ed. S. F. Morse (New York, 1957) and a collection of Stevens' critical prose, *The Necessary Angel* (New

York, 1951). A useful book of criticism is William Van O'Connor, *The Shaping Spirit* (Chicago, 1950). Critical interest in Stevens has been lively; a little search of the annual bibliography in *PMLA* for the five years after his death would comb out half a dozen first-rate articles. The discussions by R. P. Blackmur in *Language as Gesture* (New York, 1952) have been influential. A recent study is Robert Pack, *Wallace Stevens* (Rutgers University, 1958).

## *Domination of Black*

At night, by the fire,
The colors of the bushes
And of the fallen leaves,
Repeating themselves,
Turned in the room,
Like the leaves themselves
Turning in the wind.
Yes: but the color of the heavy hemlocks
Came striding.
And I remembered the cry of the peacocks.

The colors of their tails
Were like the leaves themselves
Turning in the wind,
In the twilight wind.
They swept over the room,
Just as they flew from the boughs of the hemlocks
Down to the ground.
I heard them cry—the peacocks.
Was it a cry against the twilight
Or against the leaves themselves
Turning in the wind,
Turning as the flames
Turned in the fire,
Turning as the tails of the peacocks
Turned in the loud fire,
Loud as the hemlocks
Full of the cry of the peacocks?
Or was it a cry against the hemlocks?

Out of the window,
I saw how the planets gathered

Like the leaves themselves
Turning in the wind.
I saw how the night came,
Came striding like the color of the heavy hemlocks
I felt afraid.
And I remembered the cry of the peacocks.

## Disillusionment of Ten O'Clock

THE houses are haunted
By white night-gowns.
None are green,
Or purple with green rings,
Or green with yellow rings,
Or yellow with blue rings.
None of them are strange,
With socks of lace
And beaded ceintures.
People are not going
To dream of baboons and periwinkles.
Only, here and there, an old sailor,
Drunk and asleep in his boots,
Catches tigers
In red weather.

## Sunday Morning

### I

COMPLACENCIES of the peignoir, and late
Coffee and oranges in a sunny chair,
And the green freedom of a cockatoo
Upon a rug mingle to dissipate
The holy hush of ancient sacrifice.

She dreams a little, and she feels the dark
Encroachment of that old catastrophe,
As a calm darkens among water-lights.
The pungent oranges and bright, green wings
Seem things in some procession of the dead,
Winding across wide water, without sound.
The day is like wide water, without sound,
Stilled for the passing of her dreaming feet
Over the seas, to silent Palestine,
Dominion of the blood and sepulchre.

## II

Why should she give her bounty to the dead?
What is divinity if it can come
Only in silent shadows and in dreams?
Shall she not find in comforts of the sun,
In pungent fruit and bright, green wings, or else
In any balm or beauty of the earth,
Things to be cherished like the thought of heaven?
Divinity must live within herself:
Passions of rain, or moods in falling snow;
Grievings in loneliness, or unsubdued
Elations when the forest blooms; gusty
Emotions on wet roads on autumn nights;
All pleasures and all pains, remembering
The bough of summer and the winter branch.
These are the measures destined for her soul.

## III

Jove in the clouds had his inhuman birth.
No mother suckled him, no sweet land gave
Large-mannered motions to his mythy mind.
He moved among us, as a muttering king,
Magnificent, would move among his hinds,

Until our blood, commingling, virginal,
With heaven, brought such requital to desire
The very hinds discerned it, in a star.
Shall our blood fail? Or shall it come to be
The blood of paradise? And shall the earth
Seem all of paradise that we shall know?
The sky will be much friendlier then than now,
A part of labor and a part of pain,
And next in glory to enduring love,
Not this dividing and indifferent blue.

#### IV

She says, 'I am content when wakened birds,
Before they fly, test the reality
Of misty fields, by their sweet questionings;
But when the birds are gone, and their warm fields
Return no more, where, then, is paradise?'
There is not any haunt of prophecy,
Nor any old chimera of the grave,
Neither the golden underground, nor isle
Melodious, where spirits gat them home,
Nor visionary south, nor cloudy palm
Remote on heaven's hill, that has endured
As April's green endures; or will endure
Like her remembrance of awakened birds,
Or her desire for June and evening, tipped
By the consummation of the swallow's wings.

#### V

She says, 'But in contentment I still feel
The need of some imperishable bliss.'
Death is the mother of beauty; hence from her,
Alone, shall come fulfilment to our dreams
And our desires. Although she strews the leaves
Of sure obliteration on our paths,

The path sick sorrow took, the many paths
Where triumph rang its brassy phrase, or love
Whispered a little out of tenderness,
She makes the willow shiver in the sun
For maidens who were wont to sit and gaze
Upon the grass, relinquished to their feet.
She causes boys to pile new plums and pears
On disregarded plate. The maidens taste
And stray impassioned in the littering leaves.

### VI

Is there no change of death in paradise?
Does ripe fruit never fall? Or do the boughs
Hang always heavy in that perfect sky,
Unchanging, yet so like our perishing earth,
With rivers like our own that seek for seas
They never find, the same receding shores
That never touch with inarticulate pang?
Why set the pear upon those river-banks
Or spice the shores with odors of the plum?
Alas, that they should wear our colors there,
The silken weavings of our afternoons,
And pick the strings of our insipid lutes!
Death is the mother of beauty, mystical,
Within whose burning bosom we devise
Our earthly mothers waiting, sleeplessly.

### VII

Supple and turbulent, a ring of men
Shall chant in orgy on a summer morn
Their boisterous devotion to the sun,
Not as a god, but as a god might be,
Naked among them, like a savage source.
Their chant shall be a chant of paradise,
Out of their blood, returning to the sky;

And in their chant shall enter, voice by voice,
The windy lake wherein their lord delights,
The trees, like serafin, and echoing hills,
That choir among themselves long afterward.
They shall know well the heavenly fellowship
Of men that perish and of summer morn.
And whence they came and whither they shall go
The dew upon their feet shall manifest.

## VIII

She hears, upon that water without sound,
A voice that cries, 'The tomb in Palestine
Is not the porch of spirits lingering.
It is the grave of Jesus, where he lay.'
We live in an old chaos of the sun,
Or old dependency of day and night,
Or island solitude, unsponsored, free,
Of that wide water, inescapable.
Deer walk upon our mountains, and the quail
Whistle about us their spontaneous cries;
Sweet berries ripen in the wilderness;
And, in the isolation of the sky,
At evening, casual flocks of pigeons make
Ambiguous undulations as they sink,
Downward to darkness, on extended wings.

## The Idea of Order at Key West

SHE sang beyond the genius of the sea.
The water never formed to mind or voice,
Like a body wholly body, fluttering
Its empty sleeves; and yet its mimic motion
Made constant cry, caused constantly a cry,

That was not ours although we understood,
Inhuman, of the veritable ocean.


The sea was not a mask. No more was she.
The song and water were not medleyed sound
Even if what she sang was what she heard,
Since what she sang was uttered word by word.
It may be that in all her phrases stirred
The grinding water and the gasping wind;
But it was she and not the sea we heard.


For she was the maker of the song she sang.
The ever-hooded, tragic-gestured sea
Was merely a place by which she walked to sing.
Whose spirit is this? we said, because we knew
It was the spirit that we sought and knew
That we should ask this often as she sang.


If it was only the dark voice of the sea
That rose, or even colored by many waves;
If it was only the outer voice of sky
And cloud, of the sunken coral water-walled,
However clear, it would have been deep air,
The heaving speech of air, a summer sound
Repeated in a summer without end
And sound alone. But it was more than that,
More even than her voice, and ours, among
The meaningless plungings of water and the wind,
Theatrical distances, bronze shadows heaped
On high horizons, mountainous atmospheres
Of sky and sea.

It was her voice that made
The sky acutest at its vanishing.
She measured to the hour its solitude.
She was the single artificer of the world
In which she sang. And when she sang, the sea,
Whatever self it had, became the self
That was her song, for she was the maker. Then we,
As we beheld her striding there alone,
Knew that there never was a world for her
Except the one she sang and, singing, made.

Ramon Fernandez, tell me, if you know,
Why, when the singing ended and we turned
Toward the town, tell why the glassy lights,
The lights in the fishing boats at anchor there,
As the night descended, tilting in the air,
Mastered the night and portioned out the sea,
Fixing emblazoned zones and fiery poles,
Arranging, deepening, enchanting night.

Oh! Blessed rage for order, pale Ramon,
The maker's rage to order words of the sea,
Words of the fragrant portals, dimly-starred,
And of ourselves and of our origins,
In ghostlier demarcations, keener sounds.

## Of Modern Poetry

THE poem of the mind in the act of finding
What will suffice. It has not always had
To find: the scene was set; it repeated what
Was in the script.
                    Then the theatre was changed
To something else. Its past was a souvenir.

It has to be living, to learn the speech of the place.
It has to face the men of the time and to meet
The women of the time. It has to think about war
And it has to find what will suffice. It has
To construct a new stage. It has to be on that stage
And, like an insatiable actor, slowly and
With meditation, speak words that in the ear,
In the delicatest ear of the mind, repeat,
Exactly, that which it wants to hear, at the sound
Of which, an invisible audience listens,
Not to the play, but to itself, expressed
In an emotion as of two people, as of two
Emotions becoming one. The actor is
A metaphysician in the dark, twanging
An instrument, twanging a wiry string that gives
Sounds passing through sudden rightnesses, wholly
Containing the mind, below which it cannot descend,
Beyond which it has no will to rise.
                                        It must
Be the finding of a satisfaction, and may
Be of a man skating, a woman dancing, a woman
Combing. The poem of the act of the mind.


## Thirteen Ways of Looking at a Blackbird

### I

Among twenty snowy mountains,
The only moving thing
Was the eye of the blackbird.

### II

I was of three minds,
Like a tree
In which there are three blackbirds.

### III

The blackbird whirled in the autumn winds.
It was a small part of the pantomime.

### IV

A man and a woman
Are one.
A man and a woman and a blackbird
Are one.

### V

I do not know which to prefer,
The beauty of inflections
Or the beauty of innuendoes,
The blackbird whistling
Or just after.

### VI

Icicles filled the long window
With barbaric glass.
The shadow of the blackbird
Crossed it, to and fro.
The mood
Traced in the shadow
An indecipherable cause.

### VII

O thin men of Haddam,
Why do you imagine golden birds?
Do you not see how the blackbird
Walks around the feet
Of the women about you?

### VIII

I know noble accents
And lucid, inescapable rhythms;
But I know, too,
That the blackbird is involved
In what I know.

### IX

When the blackbird flew out of sight,
It marked the edge
Of one of many circles.

### X

At the sight of blackbirds
Flying in a green light,
Even the bawds of euphony
Would cry out sharply.

### XI

He rode over Connecticut
In a glass coach.
Once, a fear pierced him,
In that he mistook
The shadow of his equipage
For blackbirds.

### XII

The river is moving.
The blackbird must be flying.

### XIII

It was evening all afternoon.
It was snowing
And it was going to snow.
The blackbird sat
In the cedar-limbs.

# WILLIAM CARLOS WILLIAMS

## Born 1883

As a modern poet must, Williams has obstinately gone his own way and created a kind of poetry which follows no rules but its own. To read him, then, demands that we "begin over" and learn the habits of this new language. His ruling objective has been to build a poetry of American speech. He regards this aim, correctly enough, as a continuation of the revolt against tradition initiated by Whitman and is probably Whitman's greatest admirer among contemporary poets. Like Whitman, he insists vigorously on the special task of the American poet, to the point of sounding a bit old-fashioned in a time when the American poet has left behind the adolescent need to stress his difference. Where Sandburg, sharing such convictions, adopted something like Whitman's manner, however, Williams has rejected Whitman's practice for one built on the "free verse" of the Imagist school that flourished briefly under Pound's leadership. He also seeks "direct treatment of the 'thing'" and the rhythm "of the musical phrase, not the metronome." He has become, among other things, a kind of modern Herrick in that, like the Imagists, he is willing to trust the exactness of his notation of some small fact to raise it without comment to poetic significance. His main concern, however, has been to render the peculiar music inherent in American speech habits and to develop without regard to the traditions of a foreign literature the forms proper to that music. Often the line divisions of his poems are little more than a device to force the reader to move through an apparently prosaic statement slowly enough to notice each of its rhythmic elements and savor its unique cadence. Like Frost, he is willing to jettison the "poetic" in order to get us to hear the poetry inherent in the actual.

Like Frost also, he risks and sometimes deserves the verdict, "This is not poetry." He is nevertheless a major poet because, on the one hand, he does often expertly discharge the obligation to lift speech into music, as the varied musical invention in even the few poems of this selection is enough to show, and, on the other, because his poems do more than capture fact, whether speech or image; they catch the glancing movements of the creating mind itself, are *psychological* notations worked up into artistic wholes, and thus hold the mirror up to a sensibility which turns out to be an unusually interesting one. "Sensibility," for Williams is not interesting as a thinker; he is as unintellectual as Whitman, and the thought in his verse, like the thought in O'Neill's plays, only exposes the author. But the vigor and subtlety with which the sensibility that controls these poems leaps from image to image, voice to voice, according to a strong subjective logic deep below the surface gives them the kind of depth and power which only a superior poet can command. The best illustration of this power cannot be included here, the early books of Williams' long poem, *Paterson,* in which in the manner of Pound's *Cantos,* by a musical interweaving of themes and images, he attempts with sometimes impressive success to create an order from the thundering chaos of his contemporary America.

Perhaps one reason for Williams' strength is the discipline of his profession, since he like Stevens has combined a career as a poet with a busy professional life. In his case he has been a doctor in Paterson, New Jersey, often working with the poorest kind of patients and seeing the biological facts

of life, as a doctor must, without a protecting veil of senti-
ment and illusion. The resulting toughness, without making
him callous, has sinewed his verse.

It is the poet's function, he writes, "to lift, by use of his
imagination and the language he hears, the material condi-
tions and appearances of his environment to the sphere of
the intelligence where they will have new currency." And
again, "It isn't what he says that counts as a work of art,
it's what he makes, with such intensity of perception that
it lives with an intrinsic movement of its own to verify its
authenticity." This, as with Stevens, is a modern version
of the theory of the poet's function classic since Coleridge.
It has seldom been applied more uncompromisingly. If
American poetry has a future, the road to it is likely to lead
through Williams.

BIBLIOGRAPHY: Most of Williams' poems appear in two volumes,
*The Collected Earlier Poems* and *The Collected Later Poems* (New
Directions: Norfolk, Conn., 1950–51); the *Later Poems,* however,
do not include the latest poems. Worth notice also are a book
of essays on American culture, *In the American Grain* (Norfolk,
Conn., 1925), *Make Light of It: Collected Stories* (New York, 1950),
and Williams' novels, *White Mule* and *In the Money. Paterson*
is in course of publication by New Directions. There is also a
*Selected Poems,* with a good introduction by Randall Jarrell (1949),
and a useful critical work by Vivienne Koch (1951). Edith Heal
has edited a collection of Williams' self-criticism, *I Wanted To
Write a Poem* (Boston, 1958).

## *Tract*

I WILL teach you my townspeople
how to perform a funeral—
for you have it over a troop
of artists—
unless one should scour the world—
you have the ground sense necessary.

See! the hearse leads.
I begin with a design for a hearse.
For Christ's sake not black—
nor white either—and not polished!
Let it be weathered—like a farm wagon—
with gilt wheels (this could be
applied fresh at small expense)
or no wheels at all:
a rough dray to drag over the ground.

Knock the glass out!
My God—glass, my townspeople!
For what purpose? Is it for the dead
to look out or for us to see
how well he is housed or to see
the flowers or the lack of them—
or what?
To keep the rain and snow from him?
He will have a heavier rain soon:
pebbles and dirt and what not.
Let there be no glass—
and no upholstery phew!
and no little brass rollers
and small easy wheels on the bottom—
my townspeople what are you thinking of?

WILLIAM CARLOS WILLIAMS · 117

A rough plain hearse then
with gilt wheels and no top at all.
On this the coffin lies
by its own weight.

              No wreaths please—
especially no hot house flowers.
Some common memento is better,
something he prized and is known by:
his old clothes—a few books perhaps—
God knows what! You realize
how we are about these things
my townspeople—
something will be found—anything
even flowers if he had come to that.
So much for the hearse.


For heaven's sake though see to the driver!
Take off the silk hat! In fact
that's no place at all for him—
up there unceremoniously
dragging our friend out to his own dignity!
Bring him down—bring him down!
Low and inconspicuous! I'd not have him ride
on the wagon at all—damn him—
the undertaker's understrapper!
Let him hold the reins
and walk at the side
and inconspicuously too!


Then briefly as to yourselves:
Walk behind—as they do in France,
seventh class, or if you ride

Hell take curtains! Go with some show
of inconvenience; sit openly—
to the weather as to grief.
Or do you think you can shut grief in?
What—from us? We who have perhaps
nothing to lose? Share with us
share with us—it will be money
in your pockets.
                        Go now
I think you are ready.


## El Hombre

IT'S a strange courage
you give me ancient star:

Shine alone in the sunrise
toward which you lend no part!


## To Waken an Old Lady

OLD age is
a flight of small
cheeping birds
skimming
bare trees
above a snow glaze.
Gaining and failing
they are buffetted
by a dark wind—
But what?

On harsh weedstalks
the flock has rested,
the snow
is covered with broken
seedhusks
and the wind tempered
by a shrill
piping of plenty.


## The Widow's Lament in Springtime

SORROW is my own yard
where the new grass
flames as it has flamed
often before but not
with the cold fire
that closes round me this year.
Thirtyfive years
I lived with my husband.
The plumtree is white today
with masses of flowers.
Masses of flowers
load the cherry branches
and color some bushes
yellow and some red
but the grief in my heart
is stronger than they
for though they were my joy
formerly, today I notice them
and turn away forgetting.
Today my son told me
that in the meadows,

at the edge of the heavy woods
in the distance, he saw
trees of white flowers.
I feel that I would like
to go there
and fall into those flowers
and sink into the marsh near them.


### Poem

As the cat
climbed over
the top of

the jamcloset
first the right
forefoot

carefully
then the hind
stepped down

into the pit of
the empty
flowerpot


### The Sea-Elephant

TRUNDLED from
the strangeness of the sea—
a kind of
heaven—

Ladies and Gentlemen!
the greatest
sea-monster ever exhibited
alive

the gigantic
sea-elephant—O wallow
of flesh where
are

there fish enough for
that
appetite stupidity
cannot lessen?

Sick
of April's smallness
the little
leaves—

Flesh has lief of you
enormous sea—
Speak!
Blouaugh! (feed

me) my
flesh is riven—
fish after fish into his maw
unswallowing

to let them glide down
gulching back
half spittle half
brine

the
troubled eyes—torn
from the sea.
(In

a practical voice) They
ought
to put it back where
it came from.

Gape.
Strange head—
told by old sailors—
rising

bearded
to the surface—and
the only
sense out of them

is that woman's
Yes
it's wonderful but they
ought to

put it
back into the sea where
it came from.
Blouaugh!

Swing—ride
walk
on wires—toss balls
stoop and

contort yourselves—
But I
am love. I am
from the sea—

Blouaugh!
there is no crime save
the too heavy
body

the sea
held playfully—comes
to the surface
the water

boiling
about the head the cows
scattering
fish dripping from

the bounty
of ... and Spring
they say
Spring is icummen in—


## The Yachts

contend in a sea which the land partly encloses
shielding them from the too heavy blows
of an ungoverned ocean which when it chooses

tortures the biggest hulls, the best man knows
to pit against its beatings, and sinks them pitilessly.
Mothlike in mists, scintillant in the minute

brilliance of cloudless days, with broad bellying sails
they glide to the wind tossing green water
from their sharp prows while over them the crew crawls

ant like, solicitously grooming them, releasing,
making fast as they turn, lean far over and having
caught the wind again, side by side, head for the mark.

In a well guarded arena of open water surrounded by
lesser and greater craft which, sycophant, lumbering
and flittering follow them, they appear youthful, rare

as the light of a happy eye, live with the grace
of all that in the mind is feckless, free and
naturally to be desired. Now the sea which holds them

is moody, lapping their glossy sides, as if feeling
for some slightest flaw but fails completely.
Today no race. Then the wind comes again. The yachts

move, jockeying for a start, the signal is set and they
are off. Now the waves strike at them but they are too
well made, they slip through, though they take in canvas.

Arms with hands grasping seek to clutch at the prows.
Bodies thrown recklessly in the way are cut aside.
It is a sea of faces about them in agony, in despair

until the horror of the race dawns staggering the mind,
the whole sea become an entanglement of watery bodies
lost to the world bearing what they cannot hold. Broken,

beaten, desolate, reaching from the dead to be taken up
they cry out, failing, failing! their cries rising
in waves still as the skillful yachts pass over.

## The Term

A RUMPLED sheet
of brown paper
about the length

and apparent bulk
of a man was
rolling with the

wind slowly over
and over in
the street as

a car drove down
upon it and
crushed it to

the ground. Unlike
a man it rose
again rolling

with the wind over
and over to be as
it was before.


## The Dance

IN Breughel's great picture, The Kermess,
the dancers go round, they go round and
around, the squeal and the blare and the
tweedle of bagpipes, a bugle and fiddles

tipping their bellies (round as the thick-
sided glasses whose wash they impound)
their hips and their bellies off balance
to turn them. Kicking and rolling about
the Fair Grounds, swinging their butts, those
shanks must be sound to bear up under such
rollicking measures, prance as they dance
in Breughel's great picture, The Kermess.

# EZRA POUND

### Born 1885

Pound's career holds a special fascination for the modern literary mind, perhaps because it illustrates both what the modern poet desires and what he fears. Abandoning a position as language instructor in Wabash College, Indiana, he settled in London in 1907, not to return to the United States for thirty-eight years (except for one brief visit) and then under duress. In the next decade he was in the vanguard of poetic progress, writing some of the best new verse himself and tirelessly and brilliantly discovering and encouraging new talent. Almost every poet reaching literary maturity at that time warmly acknowledges some sort of debt to Pound. He went into a "second exile" at the end of World War I and after four years in Paris settled in Italy. As the world moved into depression and the spread of Fascism, his alienation from his own world increased until he found himself during the Second World War broadcasting attacks on the war effort of the Allies. Captured and humiliatingly treated by American soldiers during the invasion of Italy, he was brought back to the United States to be tried for treason but was instead committed to an insane asylum, where he lived, wrote, and held a kind of rump court for thirteen years. Released in 1958, he then returned to Italy. Perhaps in his own work, and certainly in his influence on the work of others, his name will survive as long as modern poetry; in his rootlessness and symbolic fate he has enacted a basic fear which the modern artist everywhere must feel.

Since Pound was a born teacher, a vigorous and original student and critic of the craft of verse, as is still apparent

in his letters and other *obiter dicta,* the best statement of
the direction his influence took is a selection from his own
words:

> Use no superfluous word, no adjective, which does not reveal
> something.
> Don't use such an expression as 'dim lands *of peace.*' It dulls
> the image. It mixes an abstraction with the concrete. It comes
> from the writer's not realizing that the natural object is always
> the *adequate* symbol.
> Go in fear of abstraction. ...
>
> It is not necessary that a poem should rely on its music, but
> if it does rely on its music that music must be such as will
> delight the expert.
> Let the neophyte know assonance and alliteration, rhyme
> immediate and delayed, simple and polyphonic, as a musi-
> cian would expect to know harmony and counterpoint and
> all the minutiae of his craft. No time is too great to give to
> these matters or to any one of them, even if the artist seldom
> have need of them. ...
>
> My pawing over the ancients and semi-ancients has been
> one struggle to find out what has been done, once for all,
> better than it can ever be done again, and to find out what
> remains for us to do, and plenty does remain, for if we still
> feel the same emotions as those which launched the thousand
> ships, it is quite certain that we come on these feelings dif-
> ferently, through different nuances, by different intellectual
> gradations. Each age has its own abounding gifts, yet only
> some ages transmute them into matter of duration. No good
> poetry is ever written in a manner twenty years old, for to
> write in such a manner shows conclusively that the writer
> thinks from books, convention and *cliché,* and not from life,
> yet a man feeling the divorce of life and his art may naturally
> try to resurrect a forgotten mode if he find in that mode some
> leaven, or if he think he sees in it some element lacking in
> contemporary art which might unite that art again to its
> sustenance, life.
>
> As to Twentieth century poetry, ... it will, I think, move
> against poppy-cock, it will be harder and saner, it will be

EZRA POUND · 129

what Mr. Hewlett calls 'nearer the bone.' It will be as much like granite as it can be, its force will lie in its truth, its interpretative power (of course, poetic force does always rest there); I mean it will not try to seem forcible by rhetorical din, and luxurious riot. We will have fewer painted adjectives impeding the shock and stroke of it. At least for myself, I want it so, austere, direct, free from emotional slither.

These remarks make clear the reason why this proponent of a new and original poetry should have been in much of his work an imitator and translator. The aim is always to catch a fresh rhythm or effect that will permit the twentieth-century poet to unite his art again to life. His translations, in particular, are now winning increasing recognition for their extraordinary success in rendering the spirit of the poetry of remote times and lands into English. The fact that Pound, an impatient and arrogant man, often did not know very well the language from which he was translating and committed many "howlers" does not lessen his achievement, one beyond the reach of much more conscientious scholars.

His influence, exercised always in the direction of precision, concreteness, and rhythmic artistry, has been toward the primary sources of most great poetry and has thus been a most fruitful one. Its chief effect has been to convince the modern poet that a poem must justify itself at every point by its objective "presentation" and its music; it must not mean but be. Exactly fitted to the short lyric, it is not so clear that Pound's austere stress on the adequacy of the symbol, without logical connectives, is adaptable to longer forms. The chief example here, Eliot's *The Waste Land* (which Pound sharply cut in the interests of concentration with results so satisfactory to Eliot that he dedicated the poem to Pound, "the better craftsman"), though certainly not a collection of disjointed fragments, cannot easily be shown to have a greater unity than, say, Tennyson's *In Me-*

*moriam.* The difficulty is much more obvious with the most ambitious attempt yet to write a long poem according to these principles, Pound's own *The Cantos.* This lifework, though unfinished, now numbers more cantos than Dante's *Divine Comedy,* and one can already guess that, for all the fascination of its interweaving themes and echoes, its "complex unity" will be nearly indistinguishable from the kind of pattern the human mind insists on seeing in any random distribution of elements.

The obvious comparison to Eliot brings out both Pound's strength and weakness. That Eliot's poetry has succeeded to an important degree because he has worked along lines parallel to those laid down by Pound is plain to anyone who will examine his verse. The basic principles of his verse—the presentation of an "objective correlative," the appeal to the "auditory imagination," the reflection of a modern sensibility, the respect for tradition and the intensive search for those elements of the past that have relevance to the present—all correspond to similar emphases in Pound. Yet Pound himself, "the better craftsman," has achieved less. The reason usually suggested is that Eliot has dedicated his craft to the service of a personal commitment, while Pound has remained essentially egocentric and aimless. One concludes that *expertise* is not enough. True as it may be, however, this popular moral ignores not merely the dubious elements in Eliot's position but also Pound's lifelong loyalty to a second principle, the "only morality" of the poet as poet: nothing counts but excellence.

BIBLIOGRAPHY: *Personae: The Collected Poems,* Pound's earlier poems, *The Cantos, Selected Poems, Selected Essays,* and *Selected Translations* have all been brought out by New Directions, New York. A useful recent volume is M. L. Rosenthal, *A Primer of Ezra Pound* (New York, 1960). See also *Motive and Method in* The

Cantos *of Ezra Pound,* ed. Lewis Leary (Oxford, 1953, New York, 1954); Harold H. Watts, *Ezra Pound and the Cantos* (Chicago, 1952); Alice S. Amdur, *The Poetry of Ezra Pound* (Cambridge, Mass., 1936); the articles collected in *Examination of Ezra Pound,* ed. P. Russell (1950); and chapters in F. R. Leavis, *New Bearings in English Poetry* (London, 1932) and R. P. Blackmur, *Language as Gesture* (1952). Documents concerning the treason trial and its aftermath are collected in *A Casebook on Ezra Pound,* edited by William Van O'Connor and Edward Stone (New York, 1959).

# The Seafarer

### From the Anglo-Saxon

MAY I for my own self song's truth reckon,
Journey's jargon, how I in harsh days
Hardship endured oft.
Bitter breast-cares have I abided,
Known on my keel many a care's hold,
And dire sea-surge, and there I oft spent
Narrow nightwatch nigh the ship's head
While she tossed close to cliffs. Coldly afflicted,
My feet were by frost benumbed.
Chill its chains are; chafing sighs
Hew my heart round and hunger begot
Mere-weary mood. Lest man know not
That he on dry land loveliest liveth,
List how I, care-wretched, on ice-cold sea,
Weathered the winter, wretched outcast
Deprived of my kinsmen;
Hung with hard ice-flakes, where hail-scur flew,
There I heard naught save the harsh sea
And ice-cold wave, at whiles the swan cries,
Did for my games the gannet's clamour,
Sea-fowls' loudness was for me laughter,
The mews' singing all my mead-drink.
Storms, on the stone-cliffs beaten, fell on the stern
In icy feathers; full oft the eagle screamed
With spray on his pinion.
                              Not any protector
May make merry man faring needy.
This he little believes, who aye in winsome life
Abides 'mid burghers some heavy business,
Wealthy and wine-flushed, how I weary oft
Must bide above brine.

Neareth nightshade, snoweth from north,
Frost froze the land, hail fell on earth then,
Corn of the coldest. Nathless there knocketh now
The heart's thought that I on high streams
The salt-wavy tumult traverse alone.
Moaneth alway my mind's lust
That I fare forth, that I afar hence
Seek out a foreign fastness.
For this there's no mood-lofty man over earth's midst,
Not though he be given his good, but will have in his
      youth greed;
Nor his deed to the daring, nor his king to the faithful
But shall have his sorrow for sea-fare
Whatever his lord will.
He hath not heart for harping, nor in ring-having
Nor winsomeness to wife, nor world's delight
Nor any whit else save the wave's slash,
Yet longing comes upon him to fare forth on the water.
Bosque taketh blossom, cometh beauty of berries,
Fields to fairness, land fares brisker,
All this admonisheth man eager of mood,
The heart turns to travel so that he then thinks
On flood-ways to be far departing.
Cuckoo calleth with gloomy crying,
He singeth summerward, bodeth sorrow,
The bitter heart's blood. Burgher knows not—
He the prosperous man—what some perform
Where wandering them widest draweth.
So that but now my heart burst from my breastlock,
My mood 'mid the mere-flood,
Over the whale's acre, would wander wide.
On earth's shelter cometh oft to me,
Eager and ready, the crying lone-flyer,
Whets for the whale-path the heart irresistibly,

O'er tracks of ocean; seeing that anyhow
My lord deems to me this dead life
On loan and on land, I believe not
That any earth-weal eternal standeth
Save there be somewhat calamitous
That, ere a man's tide go, turn it to twain.
Disease or oldness or sword-hate
Beats out the breath from doom-gripped body.
And for this, every earl whatever, for those speaking
    after—
Laud of the living, boasteth some last word,
That he will work ere he pass onward,
Frame on the fair earth 'gainst foes his malice,
Daring ado, . . .
So that all men shall honour him after
And his laud beyond them remain 'mid the English,
Aye, for ever, a lasting life's-blast,
Delight 'mid the doughty.
                  Days little durable,
And all arrogance of earthen riches,
There come now no kings nor Cæsars
Nor gold-giving lords like those gone.
Howe'er in mirth most magnified,
Whoe'er lived in life most lordliest,
Drear all this excellence, delights undurable!
Waneth the watch, but the world holdeth.
Tomb hideth trouble. The blade is layed low.
Earthly glory ageth and seareth.
No man at all going the earth's gait,
But age fares against him, his face paleth,
Grey-haired he groaneth, knows gone companions,
Lordly men, are to earth o'ergiven,
Nor may he then the flesh-cover, whose life ceaseth,
Nor eat the sweet nor feel the sorry,

d nor think in mid heart,
e strew the grave with gold,
ers, their buried bodies
reasure hoard.

## A Pact

I MAKE a pact with you, Walt Whitman—
I have detested you long enough.
I come to you as a grown child
Who has had a pig-headed father;
I am old enough now to make friends.
It was you that broke the new wood,
Now is a time for carving.
We have one sap and one root—
Let there be commerce between us.

## In a Station of the Metro

THE apparition of these faces in the crowd;
Petals on a wet, black bough.

## The River Merchant's Wife: A Letter

WHILE my hair was still cut straight across my forehead
I played about the front gate, pulling flowers.
You came by on bamboo stilts, playing horse,
You walked about my seat, playing with blue plums.
And we went on living in the village of Chokan:
Two small people, without dislike or suspicion.

At fourteen I married My Lord you.
I never laughed, being bashful.
Lowering my head, I looked at the wall.
Called to, a thousand times, I never looked back.

At fifteen I stopped scowling,
I desired my dust to be mingled with yours
Forever and forever and forever.
Why should I climb the look out?

At sixteen you departed,
You went into far Ku-to-yen, by the river of swirling
    eddies,
And you have been gone five months.
The monkeys make sorrowful noise overhead.

You dragged your feet when you went out.
By the gate now, the moss is grown, the different mosses,
Too deep to clear them away!
The leaves fall early this autumn, in wind.
The paired butterflies are already yellow with August
Over the grass in the West garden;
They hurt me. I grow older.
If you are coming down through the narrows of the river
    Kiang,
Please let me know beforehand,
And I will come out to meet you
          As far as Cho-fu-Sa.     *By Rihaku*

## From *Hugh Selwyn Mauberley*

E.P. ODE POUR L'ÉLECTION DE SON SÉPULCHRE

FOR three years, out of key with his time,
He strove to resuscitate the dead art
Of poetry; to maintain 'the sublime'
In the old sense. Wrong from the start—

No hardly, but, seeing he had been born
In a half savage country, out of date;
Bent resolutely on wringing lilies from the acorn;
Capaneus; trout for factitious bait;

Ἴδμεν γάρ τοι πάνθ', ὅσ' ἐνι Τροίη
Caught in the unstopped ear;
Giving the rocks small lee-way
The chopped seas held him, therefore, that year.

His true Penelope was Flaubert,
He fished by obstinate isles;
Observed the elegance of Circe's hair
Rather than the mottoes on sun-dials.

Unaffected by 'the march of events,'
He passed from men's memory in *l'an trentiesme*
*De son eage;* the case presents
No adjunct to the Muses' diadem.

## Canto II

HANG it all, Robert Browning,
        there can be but the one 'Sordello.'
But Sordello, and my Sordello?
Lo Sordels si fo di Mantovana.
So-shu churned in the sea.
Seal sports in the spray-whited circles of cliff-wash,
Sleek head, daughter of Lir,
        eyes of Picasso
Under black fur-hood, lithe daughter of Ocean;
And the wave runs in the beach-groove:

'Eleanor, ἑλέναυς and ἑλέπτολις!'
          And poor old Homer blind, blind, as a bat,
Ear, ear for the sea-surge, murmur of old men's voices:
'Let her go back to the ships,
Back among Grecian faces, lest evil come on our own,
Evil and further evil, and a curse cursed on our children,
Moves, yes she moves like a goddess
And has the face of a god
          and the voice of Schoeney's daughters,
And doom goes with her in walking,
Let her go back to the ships,
          back among the Grecian voices.'
And by the beach-run, Tyro,
          Twisted arms of the sea-god,
Lithe sinews of water, gripping her, cross-hold,
And the blue-gray glass of the wave tents them,
Glare azure of water, cold-welter, close cover.
Quiet sun-tawny sand-stretch,
The gulls broad out their wings,
          nipping between the splay feathers;
Snipe come for their bath,
          bend out their wing-joints,
Spread wet wings to the sun-film,
And by Scios,
          to left of the Naxos passage,
Naviform rock overgrown,
          algæ cling to its edge,
There is a wine-red glow in the shallows,
          a tin flash in the sun-dazzle.

The ship landed in Scios,
          men wanting spring-water,
And by the rock-pool a young boy loggy with vine-must,
          'To Naxos? Yes, we'll take you to Naxos,

Cum' along, lad.' 'Not that way!'
'Aye, that way is Naxos.'
      And I said: 'It's a straight ship.'
And an ex-convict out of Italy
      knocked me into the fore-stays,
(He was wanted for manslaughter in Tuscany)
      And the whole twenty against me,
Mad for a little slave money.
      And they took her out of Scios
And off her course ...
      And the boy came to, again, with the racket,
And looked out over the bows,
      and to eastward, and to the Naxos passage.
God-sleight then, god-sleight:
      Ship stock fast in sea-swirl,
Ivy upon the oars, King Pentheus,
      grapes with no seed but sea-foam,
Ivy in scupper-hole.
Aye, I, Accœtes, stood there,
      and the god stood by me,
Water cutting under the keel,
Sea-break from stern forrards,
      wake running off from the bow,
And where was gunwale, there now was vine-trunk,
And tenthril where cordage had been,
      grape-leaves on the rowlocks,
Heavy vine on the oarshafts,
And, out of nothing, a breathing,
      hot breath on my ankles,
Beasts like shadows in glass,
      a furred tail upon nothingness.
Lynx-purr, and heathery smell of beasts,
      where tar smell had been,

Sniff and pad-foot of beasts,
   eye-glitter out of black air.
The sky overshot, dry, with no tempest,
Sniff and pad-foot of beasts,
   fur brushing my knee-skin,
Rustle of airy sheaths,
   dry forms in the *æther*.
And the ship like a keel in ship-yard,
   slung like an ox in smith's sling,
Ribs stuck fast in the ways,
   grape-cluster over pin-rack,
   void air taking pelt.
Lifeless air become sinewed,
   feline leisure of panthers,
Leopards sniffing the grape shoots by scupper-hole,
Crouched panthers by fore-hatch,
And the sea blue-deep about us,
   green-ruddy in shadows,
And Lyæus: 'From now, Accœtes, my altars,
Fearing no bondage,
   fearing no cat of the wood,
Safe with my lynxes,
   feeding grapes to my leopards,
Olibanum is my incense,
   the vines grow in my homage.'


The back-swell now smooth in the rudder-chains,
Black snout of a porpoise
   where Lycabs had been,
Fish-scales on the oarsmen.
   And I worship.
I have seen what I have seen.
   When they brought the boy I said:

'He has a god in him,
> though I do not know which god.'
And they kicked me into the fore-stays.
I have seen what I have seen:
> Medon's face like the face of a dory,
Arms shrunk into fins. And you, Pentheus,
Had as well listen to Tiresias, and to Cadmus,
> or your luck will go out of you.
Fish-scales over groin muscles,
> lynx-purr amid sea . . .
And of a later year,
> pale in the wine-red algæ,
If you will lean over the rock,
> the coral face under wave-tinge,
Rose-paleness under water-shift,
> Ileuthyeria, fair Dafne of sea-bords,
The swimmer's arms turned to branches,
Who will say in what year,
> fleeing what band of tritons,
The smooth brows, seen, and half seen,
> now ivory stillness.


And So-shu churned in the sea, So-shu also,
> using the long moon for a churn-stick . . .
Lithe turning of water,
> sinews of Poseidon,
Black azure and hyaline,
> glass wave over Tyro,
Close cover, unstillness,
> bright welter of wave-cords,
Then quiet water,
> quiet in the buff sands,
Sea-fowl stretching wing-joints,
> splashing in rock-hollows and sand-hollows

In the wave-runs by the half-dune;
Glass-glint of wave in the tide-rips against sunlight,
        pallor of Hesperus,
Grey peak of the wave,
        wave, colour of grape's pulp,

Olive grey in the near,
        far, smoke grey of the rock-slide,
Salmon-pink wings of the fish-hawk
        cast grey shadows in water,
The tower like a one-eyed great goose
        cranes up out of the olive-grove,

And we have heard the fauns chiding Proteus
        in the smell of hay under the olive-trees,
And the frogs singing against the fauns
        in the half-light.
And ...

# ROBINSON JEFFERS

Born 1887

Robinson Jeffers, like Frost, has followed "the old way to be new," though in his case it has led him down a very different path. He also began as a late-romantic and then gradually worked his way through to his own style and subject matter. He also, more obviously than Frost, represents an end, not a beginning. It is less clear that he is a culmination.

Like so many poets in this book, his life has a symbolic air. The son of a teacher of theology in Pittsburgh, Pennsylvania, after an education in various American and European universities he married Una Call Kuster and on the outbreak of World War I settled at Point Sur, on the California seacoast. "When the stagecoach topped the hill from Monterey, and we looked down through pines and seafog on Carmel Bay, it was evident that we had come without knowing it to our inevitable place." Here he built with his own hands a stone house—Tor House—and near it a high stone tower overlooking the sea where he has lived in near-seclusion and written his stark and violent poems ever since.

Stone and stoneworking, the sea and the sea-cliffs, are favorite symbols in his verse. A character in a Swedish novel remarks that not even Christ could bear to look at human life from the point of view of eternity; Jeffers perhaps illustrates the point. He advocates a "natural mysticism" that derives from the Wordsworthian tradition but that expresses a modern despair rather than Wordsworth's "joy." In Spenglerian fashion, he foresees the inevitable fall of modern civilization. Better "to be few and live far apart, where none could infect another." Better yet, perhaps, to cleanse nature of the "sick microbe," man, altogether and restore the world to the sanity of rocks and stones and trees. Jeffers professes a "sadly smiling" detachment from the bitter truth he records in his poems. Actually he is an advanced sufferer from the spirit-maimed pessimism that lies in wait for the American too roughly deprived of the confidence in his own and his nation's future so ringingly proclaimed by Whitman. The O'Neill of *The Iceman Cometh,* the Henry Adams of the *Education,* the Mark Twain of *The Mysterious Stranger,* the Hemingway of *A Farewell to Arms,* the Faulkner of *The Sound and the Fury* are all further examples. More than any of these Jeffers is fixed by the serpent gaze of doom in a single posture of fascinated surrender.

Jeffers has expressed his hatred of the modern in a series of long poems on legendary themes, the chief one, *The Tower Beyond Tragedy,* being based on the Orestes story. He has also adapted Euripedes' *Medea* and *Hippolytus,* the former was very successfully produced on Broadway. He has been drawn to classic stories, presumably, by their elemental violence, since his tales are in other senses as unclassical as possible, stripping man down as they do to "the dark primitive urgings of his being," of the sort revealed by psychoanalysis. Though they have powerful moments, in their extravagance and lack of any real interest in human individuality they become monotonous. Jeffers best demonstrates his mastery of his medium in his shorter lyrics. He uses a long, apparently loose line which superficially resembles Whitman's and perhaps derives from his practice. For Whitman's chanting rhythm, however, he substitutes a slow, heaving beat appropriate to the somber meditative tone and grand natural images of his work. His ear for the quantita-

tive equivalence of unstressed syllables, and his subtle variety
of stress and cadence, perhaps partly derived from his knowl-
edge of classic metrics, which his verse often recalls, give his
lines a much greater regularity and poetic strength than the
casual reader might notice. Whatever one's reservations as
to the health and value of what Jeffers has to say, one must
concede that in his best work he has said it supremely well.

BIBLIOGRAPHY: The Modern Library has a selection entitled *Roan
Stallion, Tamar and Other Poems* (New York, 1935). There is
also a *Selected Poetry* (New York, 1938). Naturally these do not in-
clude selections from the considerable work he has done since 1938,
especially his dramatic work. Two recent studies are Radcliffe
Squires, *The Loyalties of Robinson Jeffers* (Ann Arbor, 1956), and
Mercedes C. Monjian, *Robinson Jeffers: A Study in Inhumanism*
(University of Pittsburgh, 1958).

## To His Father

CHRIST was your lord and captain all your life,
He fails the world but you he did not fail,
He led you through all forms of grief and strife
Intact, a man full-armed, he let prevail
Nor outward malice nor the worse-fanged snake
That coils in one's own brain against your calm,
That great rich jewel well guarded for his sake
With coronal age and death like quieting balm.
I Father having followed other guides
And oftener to my hurt no leader at all,
Through years nailed up like dripping panther hides
For trophies on a savage temple wall
Hardly anticipate that reverend stage
Of life, the snow-wreathed honor of extreme age.


## Boats in a Fog

SPORTS and gallantries, the stage, the arts, the antics of
    dancers,
The exuberant voices of music,
Have charm for children but lack nobility; it is bitter
    earnestness
That makes beauty; the mind
Knows, grown adult.
                        A sudden fog-drift muffled the ocean,
A throbbing of engines moved in it,
At length, a stone's throw out, between the rocks and the
    vapor,
One by one moved shadows
Out of the mystery, shadows, fishing-boats, trailing each
    other
Following the cliff for guidance,

Holding a difficult path between the peril of the sea-fog
And the foam on the shore granite.
One by one, trailing their leader, six crept by me,
Out of the vapor and into it,
The throb of their engines subdued by the fog, patient and
    cautious,
Coasting all round the peninsula
Back to the buoys in Monterey harbor. A flight of pelicans
Is nothing lovelier to look at;
The flight of the planets is nothing nobler; all the arts
    lose virtue
Against the essential reality
Of creatures going about their business among the equally
Earnest elements of nature.

## Science

MAN, introverted man, having crossed
In passage and but a little with the nature of things this
    latter century
Has begot giants; but being taken up
Like a maniac with self-love and inward conflicts cannot
    manage his hybrids.
Being used to deal with edgeless dreams,
Now he's bred knives on nature turns them also inward:
    they have thirsty points though.
His mind forebodes his own destruction;
Actæon who saw the goddess naked among leaves and his
    hounds tore him.
A little knowledge, a pebble from the shingle,
A drop from the oceans: who would have dreamed this
    infinitely little too much?

## Tor House

IF you should look for this place after a handful of
    lifetimes:
Perhaps of my planted forest a few
May stand yet, dark-leaved Australians or the coast cypress,
    haggard
With storm-drift; but fire and the axe are devils.
Look for foundations of sea-worn granite, my fingers had
    the art
To make stone love stone, you will find some remnant.
But if you should look in your idleness after ten thousand
    years:
It is the granite knoll on the granite
And lava tongue in the midst of the bay, by the mouth of
    the Carmel
River-valley, these four will remain
In the change of names. You will know it by the wild
    seafragrance of wind
Though the ocean may have climbed or retired a little;
You will know it by the valley inland that our sun and
    our moon were born from
Before the poles changed; and Orion in December
Evenings was strung in the throat of the valley like a
    lamplighted bridge.
Come in the morning you will see white gulls
Weaving a dance over blue water, the wane of the moon
Their dance-companion, a ghost walking
By daylight, but wider and whiter than any bird in the
    world.
My ghost you needn't look for; it is probably
Here, but a dark one, deep in the granite, not dancing
    on wind
With the mad wings and the day moon.

## *Hurt Hawks*

### I

THE broken pillar of the wing jags from the clotted
    shoulder,
The wing trails like a banner in defeat,
No more to use the sky forever but live with famine
And pain a few days: cat nor coyote
Will shorten the week of waiting for death, there is game
    without talons.
He stands under the oak-bush and waits
The lame feet of salvation; at night he remembers freedom
And flies in a dream, the dawns ruin it.
He is strong and pain is worse to the strong, incapacity is
    worse.
The curs of the day come and torment him
At distance, no one but death the redeemer will humble
    that head,
The intrepid readiness, the terrible eyes.
The wild God of the world is sometimes merciful to those
That ask mercy, not often to the arrogant.
You do not know him, you communal people, or you have
    forgotten him;
Intemperate and savage, the hawk remembers him;
Beautiful and wild, the hawks, and men that are dying,
    remember him.

### II

I'd sooner, except the penalties, kill a man than a hawk;
    but the great redtail
Had nothing left but unable misery
From the bone too shattered for mending, the wing that
    trailed under his talons when he moved.
We had fed him six weeks, I gave him freedom,

He wandered over the foreland hill and returned in the
    evening, asking for death,
Not like a beggar, still eyed with the old
Implacable arrogance. I gave him the lead gift in the
    twilight. What fell was relaxed,
Owl-downy, soft feminine feathers; but what
Soared: the fierce rush: the night-herons by the flooded
    river cried fear at its rising
Before it was quite unsheathed from reality.

## Rock and Hawk

HERE is a symbol in which
Many high tragic thoughts
Watch their own eyes.

This gray rock, standing tall
On the headland, where the seawind
Lets no tree grow,

Earthquake-proved, and signatured
By ages of storms: on its peak
A falcon has perched.

I think, here is your emblem
To hang in the future sky;
Not the cross, not the hive,

But this; bright power, dark peace;
Fierce consciousness joined with final
Disinterestedness;

Life with calm death; the falcon's
Realist eyes and act
Married to the massive

> Mysticism of stone,
> Which failure cannot cast down
> Nor success make proud.

## The Eye

THE Atlantic is a stormy moat, and the Mediterranean,
The blue pool in the old garden,
More than five thousand years has drunk sacrifice
Of ships and blood and shines in the sun; but here the
    Pacific:
The ships, planes, wars are perfectly irrelevant.
Neither our present blood-feud with the brave dwarfs
Nor any future world-quarrel of westering
And eastering man, the bloody migrations, greed of power,
    battle-falcons,
Are a mote of dust in the great scale-pan.
Here from this mountain shore, headland beyond stormy
    headland plunging like dolphins through the gray sea-
    smoke
Into pale sea, look west at the hill of water: it is half the
    planet: this dome, this half-globe, this bulging
Eyeball of water, arched over to Asia,
Australia and white Antarctica: those are the eyelids that
    never close; this is the staring unsleeping
Eye of the earth, and what it watches is not our wars.

## Battle (May 28, 1940)

FORESEEN for so many years: these evils, this monstrous
    violence, these massive agonies: no easier to bear.

We saw them with slow stone strides approach, everyone
    saw them; we closed our eyes against them, we looked
And they had come nearer. We ate and drank and slept, they
    came nearer. Sometimes we laughed, they were nearer.
    Now
They are here. And now a blind man foresees what follows
    them: degradation, famine, recovery and so forth, and
    the
Epidemic manias: but not enough death to serve us, not
    enough death. It would be better for men
To be few and live far apart, where none could infect
    another; then slowly the sanity of field and mountain
And the cold ocean and glittering stars might enter their
    minds.
    Another dream, another dream.
We shall have to accept certain limitations
In future, and abandon some humane dreams; only hard-
    minded, sleepless and realist, can ride this rock-slide
To new fields down the dark mountain; and we shall have
    to perceive that these insanities are normal;
We shall have to perceive that battle is a burning flower
    or like a huge music, and the dive-bomber's screaming
    orgasm
As beautiful as other passions; and that death and life are
    not serious alternatives. One has known all these things
For many years: there is greater and darker to know
In the next hundred.

And why do you cry, my dear, why do you cry?
It is all in the whirling circles of time.
If millions are born millions will die;
In bed or in battle is no great matter
In the long orbits of time.

If England goes down and Germany up
The stronger dog will still be on top.
All in the turning of time.
If civilization goes down—that
Would be an event to contemplate.
It will not be in our time, alas, my dear,
It will not be in our time.

# E. E. CUMMINGS

Born 1894

All modernist poets outrage the orthodox. Where most of them ignore such opinion, however, one has made *épater le bourgeois* into a career—the bad boy of American verse, e. e. cummings. His literary productions, from the first incredulous glimpse of the typography to the last indignant discovery of his meaning, are nicely calculated to shock conventional minds. Again, this poet's life fits his work. Son of a Harvard teacher and Boston minister, he spent three months in a French detention camp during the First World War, under suspicion of sedition, an experience treated in his first and best book of prose, *The Enormous Room,* and after the war he lived a Bohemian life in New York and Paris while he gradually established a reputation as an *avant garde* poet, painter and playwright. His successive volumes bear such titles as *&, Is 5, W, 1 × 1, EIMI* (I am), *XAIPE* (Hail), and one book has no title at all. Clearly here is a poet who has dedicated himself to Conspicuous Difference.

Those who will trouble to look twice at his nonsense will find a shrewd intelligence behind it. The typographical madness, for example, has method in it. Cummings uses typography in many poems like the interpretative marks in a musical score, to suggest how he wants them read: spaces indicate pauses, the absence of them continuity, parentheses and the lack of other punctuation enhance a delicate, suspended effect, capital letters are touches of emphasis, etc. The purpose in all this is the perfectly serious and legiti-

mate one of forcing us to read his poems as poetic perform-
ances rather than as prose statements. The same is true of his
wrenching of sense and grammar. When Cummings writes,
for instance, "Anyone lived in a pretty how town," he is
nudging us to take a second look at such well-worn words:
*How* would a town look of which we exclaim "How pretty!"?
So when he dubs the human race "manunkind" he is invit-
ing us to ask whether the usual connotations of the name for
our species do in fact still fit what man has made of man.
Cummings has exhausted his very considerable ingenuity to
get us to pay attention to the primary elements of poetry,
sound and words. His poems are five-finger exercises in the
art of reading verse.

In subject matter they are often deliberately simple.
Cummings' specialty is the renewal of the cliché. He will
take some stock poetic subject like Spring, Young Love,
or Childhood and by verbal ingenuity, without the irony
with which another modern poet would treat such a topic,
create a sophisticated modern facsimile of the "naive" lyr-
icism of Campion or Blake. His forms are also often "stock";
clear away the typographic camouflage and one may reveal
a sonnet or other traditional lyric form. Superficially the
most shocking of moderns, Cummings is actually one of
the least radical. For this reason also he is a good modern
to begin on. Led by what is familiar in him to tolerate what
is novel, one is better prepared for the "deep" innovations
of Eliot or Stevens.

In posture and subject matter Cummings might be called
the Last of the Romantic Egoists. His world is divided into
two parts: "I" (and "you") and "mostpeople." "Life, for
mostpeople," writes Cummings, "simply isn't. ... What
do mostpeople mean by 'living'? They don't mean living.
They mean the latest and closest plural approximation to

singular prenatal passivity which science, in its finite but
unbounded wisdom, has succeeded in selling their wives. ...
You and I are human beings; for whom birth is a supremely
welcome mystery, the mystery of growing: the mystery which
happens only and whenever we are faithful to ourselves. ...
Life, for eternal us, is now; and now is much too busy
being a little more than everything to seem anything, cata-
strophic included."

This is clearly a highly dramatized simplification of the
romantic division between the self and the "loveless, ever-
anxious crowd." Whereas in an original romantic like
Whitman, the "Myself" reaches out to include the world,
here it withdraws to exclude it. Cummings' "I" is a sort of
enchanted garden apart from the crowd where the self
can wall out what it dislikes and hug its uniqueness. His
poems thus fall into two parts, "innocent" hymns to the
life of the self and rough satires on "mostpeople." With
the passage of time the satire has become steadily more
nihilistic as Cummings has repeated his comprehensive
rejection. On the other hand the affirmative lyrics have
become steadily stronger, as Cummings has moved from a
fragile poetics full of vague "flowers" and "petals" to a set
of well-ordered techniques for eclipsing the prosaic denota-
tions of words and weaving his poem of the coronas of
significance that are left. Cummings' content is fixed and
narrow and, if one likes, sentimental. His "semantic wit,"
however, has no match among modern poets. And among
so many prophets of doom, such as Jeffers, it is good to
have one jaunty and affirmative figure, even when one soon
realizes that the exclusiveness of his Yes and the inclusive-
ness of his No leave little but mood to choose between him
and Jeffers, after all.

BIBLIOGRAPHY: Cummings' *Poems 1923–1954* (New York, 1954) con-

tains all but the *95 poems* since published (1958). In addition are
*The Enormous Room* (New York, 1922); his unenchanted Russian
travel diary *EIMI* (New York, 1933); and his plays, such as *Him*
(1927) and *Santa Claus* (1946). A measure of autobiography,
among other things, may be found in *i: six nonlectures* (1953),
the text of six talks given at Harvard. Edmund Wilson, ed., *The
Collected Essays of John Peale Bishop* (New York, 1948), Lloyd
Frankenberg, *Pleasure Dome* (1949), and R. P. Blackmur, *Language
as Gesture* (1952) contain helpful essays. A good introduction to
modern poetry that features Cummings is Laura Riding and Robert
Graves, *A Survey of Modernist Poetry* (London, 1927). Two recent
studies are Charles Norman, *The Magic Maker* (New York, 1958)
and Norman Friedman, *E. E. Cummings: The Art of His Poetry*
(Johns Hopkins, 1960).

## 'the hours rise up'

the hours rise up putting off stars and it is
dawn
into the street of the sky light walks scattering poems

on earth a candle is
extinguished      the city
wakes
with a song upon her
mouth having death in her eyes

and it is dawn
the world
goes forth to murder dreams....

i see in the street where strong
men are digging bread
and i see the brutal faces of
people contented hideous hopeless cruel happy

and it is day,

in the mirror
i see a frail
man
dreaming
dreams
dreams in the mirror

and it
is dusk      on earth

a candle is lighted
and it is dark.
the people are in their houses
the frail man is in his bed
the city

sleeps with death upon her mouth having a song in her eyes
the hours descend,
putting on stars....

in the street of the sky night walks scattering poems


## 'a wind has blown'

a wind has blown the rain away and blown
the sky away and all the leaves away,
and the trees stand. I think i too have known
autumn too long

          (and what have you to say,
wind wind wind—did you love somebody
and have you the petal of somewhere in your heart
pinched from dumb summer?

            O crazy daddy
of death dance cruelly for us and start

the last leaf whirling in the final brain
of air!) Let us as we have seen see
doom's integration ........ a wind has blown the rain

away and the leaves and the sky and the
trees stand:
        the trees stand. The trees,
suddenly wait against the moon's face.

# 'in Just-'

in Just-
spring      when the world is mud-
luscious the little
lame balloonman

whistles      far      and wee

and eddieandbill come
running from marbles and
piracies and it's
spring

when the world is puddle-wonderful

the queer
old balloonman whistles
far      and      wee
and bettyandisbel come dancing

from hop-scotch and jump-rope and

it's
spring
and
         the

                  goat-footed

balloonMan      whistles
far
and
wee

## 'Buffalo Bill's'

BUFFALO BILL'S
defunct
            who used to
            ride a watersmooth-silver
                            stallion
and break onetwothreefourfive pigeonsjustlikethat
                                            Jesus

he was a handsome man
                        and what i want to know is
how do you like your blueeyed boy
Mister Death

## 'Spring is like a perhaps hand'

        SPRING is like a perhaps hand
        (which comes carefully
        out of Nowhere)arranging
        a window,into which people look(while
        people stare
        arranging and changing placing
        carefully there a strange
        thing and a known thing here)and

        changing everything carefully

spring is like a perhaps
Hand in a window
 (carefully to
and fro moving New and
Old things,while
people stare carefully
moving a perhaps
fraction of flower here placing
an inch of air there)and

without breaking anything.


'*my sweet old etcetera*'

my sweet old etcetera
aunt lucy during the recent

war could and what
is more did tell you just
what everybody was fighting

for,
my sister

isabel created hundreds
(and
hundreds)of socks not to
mention shirts fleaproof earwarmers

etcetera wristers etcetera, my
mother hoped that

i would die etcetera
bravely of course my father used
to become hoarse talking about how it was
a privilege and if only he
could meanwhile my

self etcetera lay quietly
in the deep mud et

cetera
(dreaming,
et
　cetera, of
Your smile
eyes knees and of your Etcetera)




## 'anyone lived in a pretty how town'

anyone lived in a pretty how town
(with up so floating many bells down)
spring summer autumn winter
he sang his didn't he danced his did.

Women and men(both little and small)
cared for anyone not at all
they sowed their isn't they reaped their same
sun moon stars rain

children guessed(but only a few
and down they forgot as up they grew
autumn winter spring summer)
that noone loved him more by more

when by now and tree by leaf
she laughed his joy she cried his grief
bird by snow and stir by still
anyone's any was all to her

someones married their everyones
laughed their cryings and did their dance
(sleep wake hope and then)they
said their nevers they slept their dream

stars rain sun moon
(and only the snow can begin to explain
how children are apt to forget to remember
with up so floating many bells down)

one day anyone died i guess
(and noone stooped to kiss his face)
busy folk buried them side by side
little by little and was by was

all by all and deep by deep
and more by more they dream their sleep
noone and anyone earth by april
wish by spirit and if by yes.


Women and men(both dong and ding)
summer autumn winter spring
reaped their sowing and went their came
sun moon stars rain




## 'pity this busy monster, manunkind'

pity this busy monster,manunkind,


not.     Progress is a comfortable disease:
your victim(death and life safely beyond)


plays with the bigness of his littleness
—electrons deify one razorblade
into a mountainrange;lenses extend


unwish through curving wherewhen till unwish
returns on its unself.
                          A world of made
is not a world of born—pity poor flesh


and trees,poor stars and stones,but never this
fine specimen of hypermagical

ultraomnipotence.    We doctors know

a hopeless case if—listen:there's a hell
of a good universe next door;let's go

### 'o by the by'

o by the by
has anybody seen
little you-i
who stood on a green
hill and threw
his wish at blue


with a swoop and a dart
out flew his wish
(it dived like a fish
but it climbed like a dream)
throbbing like a heart
singing like a flame


blue took it my
far beyond far
and high beyond high
bluer took it your
but bluest took it our
away beyond where

what a wonderful thing
is the end of a string
(murmurs little you-i
as the hill becomes nil)
and will somebody tell
me why people let go

## 'what if a much of a which of a wind'

what if a much of a which of a wind
gives the truth to summer's lie;
bloodies with dizzying leaves the sun
and yanks immortal stars awry?
Blow king to beggar and queen to seem
(blow friend to fiend:blow space to time)
—when skies are hanged and oceans drowned,
the single secret will still be man

what if a keen of a lean wind flays
screaming hills with sleet and snow:
strangles valleys by ropes of thing
and stifles forests in white ago?
Blow hope to terror;blow seeing to blind
(blow pity to envy and soul to mind)
—whose hearts are mountains,roots are trees,
it's they shall cry hello to the spring

what if a dawn of a doom of a dream
bites this universe in two,
peels forever out of his grave
and sprinkles nowhere with me and you?
Blow soon to never and never to twice
(blow life to isn't:blow death to was)
—all nothing's only our hugest home;
the most who die,the more we live

# ROBERT LOWELL

## Born 1917

To represent the generation of poets first publishing in America during or after World War II we have chosen the New Englander, Robert Lowell. Other recent poets as interesting and more productive—Theodore Roethke, Richard Wilbur, Elizabeth Bishop, Karl Shapiro—have been passed over because none of them has achieved the commanding voice that speaks in Lowell's best verse. One mark of the good poet is his power to seize the reader with a giant hand and carry him out of himself even before he grasps what is being said. Many recent American poets are charming, deft, exciting even, but only Lowell has this kind of authority.

Robert Lowell is related to a family famous in the history of American poetry: James Russell Lowell, contemporary of Longfellow, author of the *Biglow Papers*, political satires in dialect, the Harvard *Commemoration Ode* for the Civil War dead, and of numerous other volumes of poems and essays; Amy Lowell, free verse advocate and leader of the Imagists after Pound dropped it as "Amygism," author of such popular modern classics as "Lilacs" and "Patterns." To mention these antecedents, however, is only to emphasize Robert Lowell's uniqueness. For one thing, he was for a time a Catholic, the only one in our Protestant volume, and writes from a frame of reference that transcends Yankee New England. His strong sense of the continuity of past and present uses indifferently illustrations from family tradition, from old New England, from the Middle Ages or from ancient Rome. The Puritan tradition in New England, indeed, often stands in his poems for all to which he is most hostile:

"everything that is closed, turned inward, incestuous, that blinds or binds: the Old Law, imperialism, militarism, capitalism, Calvinism, Authority, the Father, the 'proper Bostonians,' the rich who will 'do everything for the poor except get off their backs.'" Though his poems show a remarkable eye for significant detail and are rich in local color, their general tone has an apocalyptic strangeness that separates him sharply from the at-home spirit of earlier New England poets.

Yet on a second look Lowell's verse shows perhaps the deepest roots of all in the New England past. Though he has written as a Catholic, his verse has none of the brainwashed religiosity that vitiates much modern churchly art His starting point is a sense that the world, the "realm of necessity," is finally intolerable, and that we must escape into a freedom that can only be the gift of an Other, a "terrible I AM," whose contact can be intolerable too, yet whose touch is man's only hope. This sense of sin, to use the old language, is quite strikingly not shared by any other poet in this book. It *is* something Lowell shares with many moderns, some of whom, like Eliot, for example, have also turned to a traditional Church for a refuge. Lowell's version, however, shows a much more urgent sense of a common plight, is both more concrete and more impersonal than Eliot's lonely and fastidious world-nausea. It is most akin, as Lowell well knows, to the "crisis sense" of both original and neo-Calvinism. In him perhaps the deepest strain of Protestant experience, transplanted to New England by the first Puritans and brought to new flowering by descendants such as Jonathan Edwards, comes to modern expression: an abhorrence of man's natural condition, an impatience with the "shock-absorbers" of sacerdotal religion, a craving for direct salvation. The three poems in this selection all express in different ways Lowell's sense that man is lost. Other poems, equally characteristic, suggest the possibility of Grace. In Lowell, and not alone in him, the American experience comes a kind of circle, though it returns to find all changed. He dramatizes both a continuity and a discontinuity with the past.

As for the qualities of his verse, we can do no better than quote the words of Randall Jarrell:

> Mr. Lowell is a thoroughly professional poet, and the degree of intensity of his poems is equalled by their degree of organization. Inside its elaborate stanzas the poem is put together like a mosaic: the shifts of movement, the varied pauses, the alternation in the length of sentences, and the counterpoint between lines and sentences are the outer form of a subject matter that has been given a dramatic, dialectical internal organization; and it is hard to exaggerate the strength and life, the constant richness and surprise of metaphor and sound and motion, of the language itself. The organization of the poems resembles that of a great deal of traditional English poetry—especially when compared to that type of semi-imagist modern organization in which the things of a poem seem to marshal themselves like Dryden's atoms—but often this is complicated by stream-of-consciousness, dream, or dramatic-monologue types of structure. This makes the poems more difficult, but it is worth the price—many of the most valuable dramatic effects can hardly be attained inside a more logical or abstract organization. Mr. Lowell's poetry is a unique fusion of modernist and traditional poetry, and there exist side by side in it certain effects that one would have thought mutually exclusive; but it is essentially a post- or anti-modernist poetry, and as such is certain to be influential.

"One or two of these poems," Jarrell concludes, "will be read as long as men remember English."

BIBLIOGRAPHY: Lowell's last three volumes are, *Lord Weary's Castle* (1946), *The Mills of the Kavanaughs* (1951), and *Life Studies* (1959). Randall Jarrell's "From the Kingdom of Necessity," in *Poetry and the Age* (1953) is one of the few good pieces on Lowell to have been published in book form.

## The Exile's Return

THERE mounts in squalls a sort of rusty mire,
Not ice, not snow, to leaguer the Hôtel
De Ville, where braced pig-iron dragons grip
The blizzard to their rigor mortis. A bell
Grumbles when the reverberations strip
The thatching from its spire,
The search-guns click and spit and split up timber
And nick the slate roofs on the Holstenwall
Where torn-up tilestones crown the victor. Fall
And winter, spring and summer, guns unlimber
And lumber down the narrow gabled street
Past your gray, sorry and ancestral house
Where the dynamited walnut tree
Shadows a squat, old, wind-torn gate and cows
The Yankee commandant. You will not see
Strutting children or meet
The peg-leg and reproachful chancellor
With a forget-me-not in his button-hole
When the unseasoned liberators roll
Into the Market Square, ground arms before
The Rathaus; but already lily-stands
Burgeon the risen Rhineland, and a rough
Cathedral lifts its eye. Pleasant enough,
*Voi ch'entrate*, and your life is in your hands.

## The Quaker Graveyard in Nantucket
### (For Warren Winslow, Dead at Sea)

*Let man have dominion over the fishes of the sea and the
fowls of the air and the beasts and the whole earth, and
every creeping creature that moveth upon the earth.*

I

A BRACKISH reach of shoal off Madaket,—
The sea was still breaking violently and night
Had steamed into our North Atlantic Fleet,
When the drowned sailor clutched the drag-net. Light
Flashed from his matted head and marble feet,
He grappled at the net
With the coiled, hurdling muscles of his thighs:
The corpse was bloodless, a botch of reds and whites,
Its open, staring eyes
Were lustreless dead-lights
Or cabin-windows on a stranded hulk
Heavy with sand. We weight the body, close
Its eyes and heave it seaward whence it came,
Where the heel-headed dogfish barks its nose
On Ahab's void and forehead; and the name
Is blocked in yellow chalk.
Sailors, who pitch this portent at the sea
Where dreadnaughts shall confess
Its hell-bent deity,
When you are powerless
To sand-bag this Atlantic bulwark, faced
By the earth-shaker, green, unwearied, chaste
In his steel scales: ask for no Orphean lute
To pluck life back. The guns of the steeled fleet
Recoil and then repeat
The hoarse salute.

II

Whenever winds are moving and their breath
Heaves at the roped-in bulwarks of this pier,
The terns and sea-gulls tremble at your death
In these home waters. Sailor, can you hear
The Pequod's sea wings, beating landward, fall

Headlong and break on our Atlantic wall
Off 'Sconset, where the yawing S-boats splash
The bellbuoy, with ballooning spinnakers,
As the entangled, screeching mainsheet clears
The blocks: off Madaket, where lubbers lash
The heavy surf and throw their long lead squids
For blue-fish? Sea-gulls blink their heavy lids
Seaward. The winds' wings beat upon the stones,
Cousin, and scream for you and the claws rush
At the sea's throat and wring it in the slush
Of this old Quaker graveyard where the bones
Cry out in the long night for the hurt beast
Bobbing by Ahab's whaleboats in the East.

### III

All you recovered from Poseidon died
With you, my cousin, and the harrowed brine
Is fruitless on the blue beard of the god,
Stretching beyond us to the castles in Spain,
Nantucket's westward haven. To Cape Cod
Guns, cradled on the tide,
Blast the eelgrass about a waterclock
Of bilge and backwash, roil the salt and sand
Lashing earth's scaffold, rock
Our warships in the hand
Of the great God, where time's contrition blues
Whatever it was these Quaker sailors lost
In the mad scramble of their lives. They died
When time was open-eyed,
Wooden and childish; only bones abide
There, in the nowhere, where their boats were tossed
Sky-high, where mariners had fabled news
Of IS, the whited monster. What it cost
Them is their secret. In the sperm-whale's slick

I see the Quakers drown and hear their cry:
'If God himself had not been on our side,
If God himself had not been on our side,
When the Atlantic rose against us, why,
Then it had swallowed us up quick.'

### IV

This is the end of the whaleroad and the whale
Who spewed Nantucket bones on the thrashed swell
And stirred the troubled waters to whirlpools
To send the Pequod packing off to hell:
This is the end of them, three-quarters fools,
Snatching at straws to sail
Seaward and seaward on the turntail whale,
Spouting out blood and water as it rolls,
Sick as a dog to these Atlantic shoals:
*Clamavimus,* O depths. Let the sea-gulls wail

For water, for the deep where the high tide
Mutters to its hurt self, mutters and ebbs.
Waves wallow in their wash, go out and out,
Leave only the death-rattle of the crabs,
The beach increasing, its enormous snout
Sucking the ocean's side.
This is the end of running on the waves;
We are poured out like water. Who will dance
The mast-lashed master of Leviathans
Up from this field of Quakers in their unstoned graves?

### V

When the whale's viscera go and the roll
Of its corruption overruns this world
Beyond tree-swept Nantucket and Wood's Hole
And Martha's Vineyard, Sailor, will your sword

Whistle and fall and sink into the fat?
In the great ash-pit of Jehoshaphat
The bones cry for the blood of the white whale,
The fat flukes arch and whack about its ears,
The death-lance churns into the sanctuary, tears
The gun-blue swingle, heaving like a flail,
And hacks the coiling life out: it works and drags
And rips the sperm-whale's midriff into rags,
Gobbets of blubber spill to wind and weather,
Sailor, and gulls go round the stoven timbers
Where the morning stars sing out together
And thunder shakes the white surf and dismembers
The red flag hammered in the mast-head. Hide,
Our steel, Jonas Messias, in Thy side.

## VI

### OUR LADY OF WALSINGHAM

There once the penitents took off their shoes
And then walked barefoot the remaining mile;
And the small trees, a stream and hedgerows file
Slowly along the munching English lane,
Like cows to the old shrine, until you lose
Track of your dragging pain.
The stream flows down under the druid tree,
Shiloah's whirlpools gurgle and make glad
The castle of God. Sailor, you were glad
And whistled Sion by that stream. But see:

Our Lady, too small for her canopy,
Sits near the altar. There's no comeliness
At all or charm in that expressionless
Face with its heavy eyelids. As before,
This face, for centuries a memory,
*Non est species, neque decor,*

Expressionless, expresses God: it goes
Past castled Sion. She knows what God knows,
Not Calvary's Cross nor crib at Bethlehem
Now, and the world shall come to Walsingham.

### VII

The empty winds are creaking and the oak
Splatters and splatters on the cenotaph,
The boughs are trembling and a gaff
Bobs on the untimely stroke
Of the greased wash exploding on a shoal-bell
In the old mouth of the Atlantic. It's well;
Atlantic, you are fouled with the blue sailors,
Sea-monsters, upward angel, downward fish:
Unmarried and corroding, spare of flesh
Mart once of supercilious, wing'd clippers,
Atlantic, where your bell-trap guts its spoil
You could cut the brackish winds with a knife
Here in Nantucket, and cast up the time
When the Lord God formed man from the sea's slime
And breathed into his face the breath of life,
And blue-lung'd combers lumbered to the kill.
The Lord survives the rainbow of His will.

## Mother Marie Therese

### Drowned in 1912

*The speaker is a Canadian nun stationed in New Brunswick.*

OLD sisters at our Maris Stella House
Remember how the Mother's strangled grouse
And snow-shoe rabbits matched the royal glint
Of Pio Nono's vestments in the print

That used to face us, while our aching ring
Of stationary rockers saw her bring
Our cake. Often, when sunset hurt the rocks
Off Carthage, and surprised us knitting socks
For victims of the Franco-Prussian War,
Our scandal'd set her frowning at the floor;
And vespers struck like lightning through the gloom
And oaken ennui of her sitting room.
It strikes us now, but cannot re-inspire;
False, false and false, I mutter to my fire.
The good old times, ah yes! But good, that all's
Forgotten like our Province's cabals;
And Jesus, smiling earthward, finds it good;
For we were friends of Cato, not of God.
This sixtieth Christmas, I'm content to pray
For what life's shrinkage leaves from day to day;
And it's a sorrow to recall our young
Raptures for Mother, when her trophies hung,
Fresh in their blood and color, to convince
Even Probationers that Heaven's Prince,
Befriending, whispered: "Is it then so hard?
Tarry a little while, O disregard
Time's wings and armor, when it flutters down
Papal tiaras and the Bourbon crown;
For quickly, priest and prince will stand, their shields
Before each other's faces, in the fields,
Where, as I promised, virtue will compel
Michael and all his angels to repel
Satan's advances, till his forces lie
Beside the Lamb in blissful fealty."
Our Indian summer! Then, our skies could lift,
God willing; but an Indian brought the gift.
"A sword," said Father Turbot, "not a saint";
Yet He who made the Virgin without taint,

Chastised our Mother to the Rule's restraint.
Was it not fated that the sweat of Christ
Would wash the worldly serpent? Christ enticed
Her heart that fluttered, while she whipped her hounds
Into the quicksands of her manor grounds
A lordly child, her habit fleur-de-lys'd
There she dismounted, sick; with little heed,
Surrendered. Like Proserpina, who fell
Six months a year from earth to flower in hell;
She half-renounced by Candle, Book and Bell
Her flowers and fowling pieces for the Church.
She never spared the child and spoiled the birch;
And how she'd chide her novices, and pluck
Them by the ears for gabbling in Canuck,
While she was reading Rabelais from her chaise,
Or parroting the *Action Française*.
Her letter from the soi-disant French King,
And the less treasured golden wedding ring
Of her shy Bridgeroom, yellow; and the regal
Damascus shot-guns, pegged upon her eagle
Emblems from Hohenzollern standards, rust.
Our world is passing; even she, whose trust
Was in its princes, fed the gluttonous gulls,
That whiten our Atlantic, when like skulls
They drift for sewage with the emerald tide.
Perpetual novenas cannot tide
Us past that drowning. After Mother died,
"An émigrée in this world and the next,"
Said Father Turbot, playing with his text.
Where is he? Surely, he is one of those,
Whom Christ and Satan spew! But no one knows
What's happened to that porpoise-bellied priest.
He lodged with us on Louis Neuvième's Feast,
And celebrated her memorial mass.

His bald spot tapestried by colored glass,
Our angels, Prussian blue and flaking red,
He squeaked and stuttered: "N-n-nothing is so d-dead
as a dead s-s-sister." Off Saint Denis' Head,
Our Mother, drowned on an excursion, sleeps.
Her billy goat, or its descendant, keeps
Watch on a headland, and I hear it bawl
into this sixty-knot Atlantic squall,
"Mamamma's Baby," past Queen Mary's Neck,
The ledge at Carthage—almost to Quebec,
Where Monsieur de Montcalm, on Abraham's
Bosom, asleep, perceives our world that shams
His New World, lost—however it atones
For Wolfe, the Englishman, and Huron bones
And priests'. O Mother, here our snuffling crones
and cretins feared you, but I owe you flowers:
The dead, the sea's dead, has her sorrows, hours
on end to lie tossing to the east, cold,
Without bed-fellows, washed and bored and old,
Bilged by her thoughts, and worked on by the worms,
Until her fossil convent come to terms
With the Atlantic. Mother, there is room
Beyond our harbor. Past its wooden Boom
Now weak and waterlogged, that Frontenac
Once diagrammed, she welters on her back.
The bell-buoy, whom she called the Cardinal,
Dances upon her. If she hears at all,
She only hears it tolling to this shore,
Where our frost-bitten sisters know the roar
Of water, inching, always on the move
For virgins, when they wish the times were love,
And their hysterical hosannahs rouse
The loveless harems of the buck ruffed grouse,
Who drums, untroubled now, beside the sea—

As if he found our stern virginity
*Contra naturam.* We are ruinous;
God's Providence through time has mastered us:
Now all the bells are tongueless, now we freeze,
A later Advent, pruner of warped trees,
Whistles about our nunnery slabs, and yells,
And water oozes from us into wells;
A new year swells and stirs. Our narrow Bay
Freezes itself and us. We cannot say
Christ even sees us, when the ice floes toss
His statue, made by Hurons, on the cross,
That Father Turbot sank on Mother's mound—
A whirligig! Mother, we must give ground,
Little by little; but it does no good.
Tonight, while I am piling on more driftwood,
And stooping with the poker, you are here,
Telling your beads; and breathing in my ear,
You watch your orphan swording at her fears.
I feel you twitch my shoulder. No one hears
Us mock the sisters, as we used to, years
And years behind us, when we heard the spheres
Whirring *venite;* and we held our ears.
My mother's hollow sockets fill with tears.

# NOTES

## LONGFELLOW

"The Day Is Done." Written in the fall of 1844 as proem to *The Waif,* a small volume of poems of the "humbler" poets selected by Longfellow and published at Christmas of that year.

"In the Churchyard at Cambridge." Written in 1851. Negroes were held in slavery, largely for domestic service, in the northern colonies until after the Revolution. It was not usual, of course, to bury a slave in the same ground as his master or mistress.

"The Cross of Snow." Written in 1879, eighteen years after his wife's death.

p. 26  *benedight.* Blessed.

## POE

"The City in the Sea." First published in 1831 under the title "The Doomed City." Other early titles were "The City of Sin" and "The City in the Sea: a Prophecy." Beside an obvious indebtedness to Byron's "Darkness," the poem echoes Shelley ("Lines Written among the Euganean Hills"), Coleridge, a compatriot N. P. Willis, and especially the Bible (see *Revelation* 16: 18–20; *Isaiah* 14: 9). The subject can be called the dead; the sinful dead; "the interminable durability of the past"; or death as oblivion.

"The Raven," Poe's most popular poem was composed over a three-year period and published in 1845. Its germ may be found in his comment on the raven in Dickens' *Barnaby Rudge:* "Its croakings might have been *prophetically* heard in the course of the drama." For the metrical form he was indebted to Elizabeth Barrett Browning.

p. 34  *Pallas.* Pallas Athene, goddess of wisdom. Poe once planned to use an owl instead of a raven.

p. 36  *gloated.* Refracted light from (rare).

*tinkled.* "No human or physical foot could tinkle on a soft carpet," Poe acknowledged in a letter, "therefore, the tinkling of feet would vividly convey the supernatural impression." An instance of the experimentation with synesthetic effects which helped to attract the attention of Baudelaire to Poe.

*nepenthe.* Drug of forgetfulness.

p. 37 *balm in Gilead. Jeremiah* 8: 22.

*Aidenn.* Mohammedan paradise.

"Ulalume." Recent criticism has revealed that the elaborate legendary costume of this poem conceals a fairly simple personal subject. After his wife's death, Poe fell into the habit of taking night walks to her grave near New York City where he was living. The walks lay through country like that portrayed in the misty pictures of Robert Walter Weir, a Hudson River landscape painter of the day, and by ponds recalling the "Lac des Fées" of the popular ballet composer, Jean François Auber. The poem allegorizes such a walk on the first anniversary of her death. The walker is in a divided state of mind, one part, the surface consciousness, or "I," forgetful of her and hopeful of new happiness, the other deeper consciousness, or "soul," foreboding and fearful, until the sight of the tomb itself dissipates the dreams and plunges the walker back into "never-ending remembrance." The mystification of the autobiographical subject in the poem represents Poe's effort to universalize it and increase its suggestiveness. Perhaps also, it has been suggested, he was ashamed of the feelings he was treating.

p. 38 *immemorial.* That this term has the indefiniteness Poe desired is shown by consulting those who try to explain it: "beyond the grasp and scope of memory" (Alterton and Craig); "an intensive, meaning 'most memorable' " (Bradley, Beatty and Long).

*scoriac.* Of lava.

*Yaanek.* A recently discovered volcano in Antarctica. The reference carries therefore the connotation of outer cold as well as of inner fire.

p. 39 *Astarte.* Phoenician goddess of earthly love, associated both with the planet Venus and with the moon. Both, we are told, would have been "crescent" and in "the Lion" early in the morning in October and either, therefore, may be meant here. "Venus could not be seen crescent with the naked eye, but that would not have worried Poe" (Quinn).

*the worm. Isaiah* 66: 24.

*the Lion.* The sign of the zodiac Leo—a baneful influence.

## WHITMAN

"One's-Self I Sing." This and the following are among a group of introductory poems which Whitman wrote for various editions of *Leaves of Grass* and finally collected under the title "Inscriptions."

"The Ship Starting." First published in *Drum-Taps* (1865), a volume of war poems soon included in *Leaves of Grass*.

"There Was a Child." One of the original poems of 1855.

p. 47    *Third-month.* From childhood associations Whitman picked up the Quaker habit of numbering the days of the week and the months of the year. "Third-month" is of course March.

p. 48    *aureola.* The luminous area surrounding the sun when seen through mist.
*sea-crow.* A gull.

"Whoever You Are." The "me" in this poem is both book and man.

"By the Bivouac's Fitful Flame." The next three poems are from *Drum-Taps* and illustrate the more concise and objective style to which Whitman came in those poems.

"Reconciliation." Written at the close of the war.

"Sparkles from the Wheel." Both this and the previous poem were first published in 1871. James Miller has been the first to notice how the way Whitman presents and lingers over this street scene makes it grow into a moving image of the aging poet himself.

"The Dismantled Ship." Written in the last years of the poet's life.

## DICKINSON

"Safe in their Alabaster Chambers." The version printed is the original one of 1859. In 1861 Dickinson substituted another second stanza:

> Grand go the Years – in the Crescent – above them –
> Worlds scoop their Arcs –
> And Firmaments – row –
> Diadems – drop – and Doges – surrender –
> Soundless as dots – on a Disc of Snow –

"There's a certain Slant of light."

p. 61    *look of Death.* I.e., the eyes of one dead.

"The Soul selects."

p. 61   *Majority.* Coming of age.

    *be.* Dickinson has a special fondness for this usage. It hovers between the quality of a subjunctive (*Even supposing that an emperor,* etc.) and that of an intensified mode of the continuing present that might be called the sustaining present (*No matter how many times even an emperor,* etc.).

"Their Hight in Heaven." "They" is the dead, those we have loved. The poem is a comment on the conventional consolations offered the mourner at a death.

"This quiet Dust."

p. 65   *Exist an Oriental Circuit.* Live a rich cycle.

"A Route of Evanescence." Since half the pleasure in a riddle poem like this is to guess the subject, we will confine our editorial aid to one hint: the subject is not an insect.

p. 67   *Cochineal.* Carmine.

    *mail from Tunis.* Mail-rider from Africa. Dickinson is thinking of Antonio's comment about Claribel in Shakespeare's *The Tempest* (II, i, 246–48):

> She that is queen of Tunis; she that dwells
> Ten leagues beyond man's life; she that from Naples
> Can have no note, unless the sun were post . . .

"Essential Oils."

p. 67   *In Ceaseless Rosemary.* Forever in memory (only). "*Ophelia.* There's rosemary, that's for remembrance" (*Hamlet,* IV: 5). In another version Dickinson wrote "In Spiceless Sepulchre."

## ROBINSON

"Walt Whitman." Robinson omitted this poem from his collected works. Even while we can see why, it is still useful to show his feeling about a poet who might seem so unlike himself.

"Luke Havergal." The simple symbolism of this poem is explained for any careful reader by the context. The persons of the poem might cause confusion. There is only one actual person, Luke Havergal himself; the poem speaks his despair as if in a voice "out of a grave." It is convenient to think of the "I" and the "she" as two aspects in his mind of the same person, but Robinson leaves the matter mysterious, as it should be.

"How Annandale Went Out." Annandale is the central figure in other poems by Robinson; in this poem the doctor who attended his last illness is speaking. To understand him, one must imagine his gestures. The poem is a good example of the effort of Robinson, like Frost, to renew the old forms, in this case the sonnet, by bringing the language of poetry closer to actual speech.

p. 74   *a slight kind of engine.* A small instrument. Cf. Milton's "Lycidas": "And that two-handed engine at the door."

"Flammonde." A good illustration of Robinson's fondness for understatement, periphrasis, aphorism and other devices of indirection.

"Mr. Flood's Party."

p. 80   *Roland.* Hero of *La Chanson de Roland.* The reference is to his last battle, when he vainly blew his horn for rescue.

"Karma." In Buddhist philosophy, the name for the cumulative results of action; the unbroken chain of cause and effect.

# FROST

"Design." One of the classic (and most discredited) traditional arguments for a divine governance of the world is the "argument from design": the adaptation of parts of the world to each other, notably of nature to the needs of man, evidences an order or design in the world which in turn implies a Designer, as a watch implies a watchmaker.

p. 95   *white heal-all.* A common New England flower, usually blue. See line 10.

"Provide Provide."

p. 96   *Abishag.* See *I Kings* 1: 1–4.
   *occupy a throne,* etc. Perhaps a reference to Elizabeth I of England.

# STEVENS

"Domination of Black." A pattern of words "abstracted" from the subject as a cubist painting is abstracted from the geometrical shapes of a real-life scene. The pattern in this case is mobile; the basic motion is circular. The poem is still a presentation of an emotion, not "pure" poetry, but the main interest is aesthetic.

p. 102   *hemlocks . . . peacocks.* In Stevens' youth it was not uncommon for a farm in Pennsylvania, where he grew up, to keep a peacock or two in the yard. Both these details, therefore, are realistic, not fanciful.

"Disillusionment of Ten O'Clock." A good example of Stevens' color symbolism. The subject of the poem is a Blakeian contrast between reasonableness and imagination. The "sailor," of course, is metaphorical.

"Sunday Morning." One of the best examples of Stevens' mastery of the opulent, eloquent blank verse line, in the tradition of Milton, Keats, and Tennyson, which holds the reader with its rhetoric almost independently of its meaning. The form is appropriate to Stevens' subject: modern religion. He is contrasting the other-worldliness of traditional Christianity, with its dreams of "imperishable bliss," to the fact that we can form no conception of any bliss except in the image of our experiences of perishable beauty. Earth is all of paradise that we shall know: "Death is the mother of beauty," in that beauty is the transient product of a natural cycle that ends in death, and that our awareness of this fact forms part of our sense of beauty. A modern paganism, then, the poem suggests, would be a better religion for us, because better fitted to the facts, than the "blood and sepulchre" of Christianity. But the argument is hardly more than a scaffolding for the poetry, which is saturated with subtleties of meaning and feeling that escape all summary. .

"The Idea of Order at Key West." The argument: the physical facts of nature (the sea) are "veritable" and "not a mask"; but the meaning of these facts, their ordering and comprehension, is the work of the human mind, which is thus "the single artificer of the world." The poem is in honor of what Coleridge called the "primary imagination," "the living Power and prime Agent of all human Perception."

p. 109 *Ramon Fernandez.* Arbitrary Spanish name, not the critic.

"Of Modern Poetry." An example of Stevens' later and more abstract manner. In contrast to the intoning of such a poem as "Sunday Morning" this is carefully and meticulously spoken, an illustration of the act of the mind which it describes. The stress here on the poem as the *act* of the mind (not the product) reflects the same pragmatic emphasis that we find in Frost and Williams and which is, indeed, central to American thought and literature of their generation if not generally.

"Thirteen Ways of Looking at a Blackbird." A deliberately cryptic piece in a pseudo-Japanese manner that is intended to tease the mind to search and guess the significance of its central symbol. If we associate the blackbird with the actuality from which "the act of the mind" in poetry must start and to which it must relate if it is to have meaning, we shall probably not be far wrong.

p. 111 *Haddam.* A town in Connecticut—a fact which seems to have no special significance.

## WILLIAMS

"Tract." First published in 1917. Funerals are managed differently now, but no better.

p. 118 *We who have . . . in your pockets.* An example of Williams' ironic indirection. The meaning is something like: Grief cannot be hoarded like wealth. It is something we all have in common. Recognize this and do not attempt to keep your grief to yourself. Humble your pride of possession and accept the equality of the grave. In this way you will enrich us and yourselves.

"The Sea-Elephant." A little drama of voices in the manner though not the spirit of Eliot's *The Waste Land.* The subject behind the subject emerges indistinctly, as the sea-elephant emerges from the water; notice, however, "But I / am love," and other such hints.

p. 121 *Flesh has lief of you.* Flesh wishes, prefers you.

p. 122 *is that woman's.* The next line starts a new voice (the "practical" one) and a new sentence. This sentence is unfinished, the statement about woman's (what?) is never made; the meaning is glimpsed and lost like what the sailors thought they saw. One resulting hint is that the practical voice is a woman's.

p. 123 *Spring is icummen in—.* An allusion to one of the earliest extant songs in English, one that opens most anthologies of English verse.

"The Yachts." Beginning as an admiring description, the poem moves suddenly as the race starts into a surrealistic vision of the "horror of the race."

## POUND

"The Seafarer." An example of Pound's brilliant translations. The alliterations, of course, are an echo of the alliterative verse of the original.

p. 132 *Mere-weary.* Sea-weary.

"In a Station of the Metro." An instance of the "Vorticism" of 1916. Pound's note: "In a poem of this sort one is trying to record the precise instant when a thing outward and objective transforms itself, or darts into a thing inward and subjective."

"The River Merchant's Wife."

Another translation, in this case from Li Po, whose name Pound gives in Japanese form.

"Hugh Selwyn Mauberley." The whole poem is Pound's "farewell to all that," before he left England for France and Italy. The sub-title of our selection echoes Mallarmé's "Le Tombeau d'Edgar Poe." "The sublime" was one of the aims of neo-classic poetry. Capaneus of Argos, in Aeschylus' *Seven against Thebes*, swore to force entrance to Thebes in spite of Zeus and was struck dead. He is the only blasphemer identified by name in Dante's *Inferno*. The Greek line ("For we know all the things that are in Troy") paraphrases the song of the sirens in *The Odyssey* XII: 189, a poem echoed several times more in succeeding lines. The French echoes the first line of Villon's *Grand Testament*.

"Canto II." As Pound once explained his purpose in *The Cantos*, "There will be no plot, no chronicle of events, no logic of discourse, but two themes, the descent into Hades from Homer, a metamorphosis from Ovid, and mixed with these medieval or modern historical characters." Canto II, Hugh Kenner writes, treats "form out of flux." "The entire Canto is concerned with the sea, Aphrodite's native element. It is the blue-gray liquid in which seals disport and snipe bathe; but the right kind of eyes bent upon its depths are rewarded with anthropomorphic glimpses, the sea-god's 'Lithe sinews of water,' or 'The smooth brows, seen, and half seen.'" The chief myth it echoes is the story of Dionysus from Ovid's *Metamorphoses*, III: 577–699. As Robert Graves summarizes it:

> Arriving at Icaria, he found that his ship was unseaworthy, and hired another from certain Tyrrhenian sailors who claimed to be bound for Naxos. But they proved to be pirates and, unaware of his godhead, steered for Asia, intending to sell him there as a slave. Dionysus made a vine grow from the deck and enfold the mast, while ivy twined about the rigging; he also turned the oars into serpents, and became a lion himself, filling the vessel with phantom beasts and the sound of flutes, so that the terrified pirates leaped overboard and became dolphins.

The foreign phrases mean: (l.4) "Sordello was from around Mantua"; (l.11) "A hell to ships, a hell to cities" (puns on "Helen" from Aeschylus' *Agamemnon*, l. 689). It would be pointless to try to explain the other allusions. As with Eliot, it is important not to fall into the trap set by the poet himself and read this poem as a kind of riddle for the erudite, but to look and listen, as with any poem, and let the clarification of the references wait until the poem has convinced one that one wants to know everything about it.

## JEFFERS

"Battle (May 28, 1940)." The date is that of the Belgian surrender to Hitler and the British evacuation of Dunkirk.

## CUMMINGS

"a wind has blown." Barring a few half-rhymes, this is a regular Shakespearean sonnet. Against the two-part form of the sonnet it plays a three-part structure, much like the ordinary form of a song in music. "The petal of somewhere" is an example of Cummings' poetry of connotations: the denotation of each word is largely canceled; nothing counts poetically but their atmospheres.

"in Just-spring." At the adjective "goat-footed," the poem slips openly into myth.

"Buffalo Bill's." Presumably a boy is speaking.

"my sweet old etcetera." This is not hard to read if we are alert to changes of voice.

"anyone lived in a pretty how town." The story is simple, once we see that "anyone" and "noone" are proper names. Rhythmic patterns are important: bells ring the cycle of time from the second line on, for instance. "By" here operates as a copula or mathematical symbol: "when by now" signifies something like "*when* to the *now* power," etc.

"pity this busy monster, manunkind." Again a sonnet. The references to electronic microscopes and huge telescopes, examples of the pointless curiosity of science, are fairly plain. The prefix "un" is a favorite of the later Cummings and is often attached to some attribute of "mostpeople" to signify its emptiness.

"o by the by." Possible subtitle: Short Happy Life of the Little Man Who Was Carried Away by a Kite.

"what if a much of a which of a wind." By startling us with grammatical double exposures—the device of substituting, in a familiar form (what if a —— of a —— of a ——, etc.), unexpected words, often the "wrong" part of speech—Cummings keeps us reminded that we are reading a poem, not a manifesto.


## LOWELL

"The Exile's Return." The time is the entry of American troops into the Rhineland during the last war. The exile is presumably a German refugee returning with the troops.

p. 172 *Voi ch'entrate.* The closing words of the inscription over Dante's Hell: Abandon all hope, you who enter.

"The Quaker Graveyard in Nantucket."

*Warren Winslow.* A cousin of Lowell's whose ship was lost during World War II.

*Let man, etc. Genesis* 1: 26.

p. 173 *dead-lights.* Heavily-glassed ship's ports.

*Ahab.* The first of many references in this poem to Melville's *Moby Dick.*

*the earth-shaker.* An epithet for Poseidon, god of the sea and the earthquake.

p. 175 *Clamavimus. Psalms* 130: 1: "Out of the depths have I cried unto thee, O Lord."

*mast-lashed master of Leviathans.* Not Ahab, who was neither, but the crucified and risen Christ.

p. 176 *ash-pit of Jehoshaphat.* The God-fearing king of Judah who opposed the wicked Ahab: see *II Kings* 9: *II Chronicles* 17–20. "The valley of judgment. The world, according to some prophets and scientists, will end in fire." (Lowell's note).

*swingle.* A flail.

*Jonas Messias.* Jonah's three days in the whale were traditionally compared to Christ's three days in the tomb.

*Our Lady of Walsingham.* Shrine of the Virgin at Walsingham, England, the object of medieval pilgrimage. "Our Lady of Walsingham is an adaptation of several paragraphs from E. I. Watkin's *Catholic Art and Culture.* The Virgin is a symbol of contemplation." (Lowell's note). There was a saying, "When England goes to Walsingham, England will return to the Church."

Shiloah. For centuries the location of the tabernacle of
Israel.

*Sion*. Hill of Jerusalem, symbol of Israel, the final gathering
place.

*Non est species, neque decor. Isaiah* 53: 2: "He hath no
form nor comeliness." (Of the Messiah).

p. 177 *cenotaph*. Empty tomb.

*bell-trap*. A stench trap, used in plumbing.

*The Lord survives, etc*. Cryptic and menacing conclusion
meaning something like: The inscrutable will and power
of the Lord survive the abrogation of His apparent will or
promise of mercy once symbolized in the rainbow.

"Mother Marie Therese."

p. 177 *Pio Nono*. Pope Pius the Ninth (1846–78).

p. 178 *Cato*. The allusion is to the implacable enemy of Carthage.
We were too politically-minded, appears to be the sense.

*Indian brought the gift*. I.e., the gift was taken back.

p. 179 *Action Française*. French royalist journal.

p. 180 *Monsieur de Montcalm, etc*. In 1759 the British under
Wolfe, by a desperate invasion of the Plains of Abraham
commanding Quebec, defeated the French under Mont-
calm, though both generals were killed, and won Canada
for England. The Hurons were Indian allies of the French.

*Frontenac*. Seventeenth century governor of Canada.

p. 181 *venite*. "Come," as in *Psalm* 94: "Come, let us praise the
Lord with joy." A very common imperative in the prayers
and responses of the Catholic service from Advent to Easter.